The fun way to SERIOUS BRIDGE

by
HARRY LAMPERT

A FIRESIDE BOOK
Published by Simon & Schuster
New York London Toronto Sydney

This is a revised edition of a book originally published
in 1978 by Hardel Publishing

Copyright © 1978, 1980 by Harry Lampert
All rights reserved
including the right of reproduction
in whole or in part in any form
First Fireside Edition, 1986
Published by Simon & Schuster, Inc.
Simon & Schuster Building
Rockefeller Center
1230 Avenue of the Americas
New York, New York 10020

Manufactured in the United States of America

40 39 38

Library of Congress Cataloging in Publication Data

ISBN-13: 978-0-671-63027-0
ISBN-10:   0-671-63027-X

*Dedicated to
my dear wife, Adele,
my favorite partner
. . . in everything.*

CONTENTS

Here I am — into my second edition of "The Fun Way to Serious Bridge." The original concept was so well received that we decided to expand the book to include a number of ideas that will be of real interest to the more experienced player as well as to the neophyte.

I had fun creating the additional cartoon illustrations. I hope they will help make the various conventions and concepts easier to understand and enjoyable as well.

But how did the whole thing begin?

I didn't start out writing a book. I started teaching bridge.

I wanted my students to understand the logic of the game—not just memorize numbers. I wanted them to understand why certain actions made sense so that they could make the proper decisions even if they momentarily forgot the "exact point-count."

This was fine in theory—but how would I do it?

Since my background included cartooning, I started using illustrations to help get across the serious principles of bridge. I tried to give my students fun associations which would remain in their minds.

I used a giant artists' pad and began sketching away. My

students laughed and, best of all, they understood the points I was making.

After a while, they began trying to copy my cartoons and asked if they could xerox the visual aids.

"But all the information is in your standard text books," I responded.

"Yes," they said," but your visuals make it simpler and we understand it better. Can you put it out in book form?"

"O.K.," I said. "I will."

So here it is — *The Fun Way to Serious Bridge.*

THE FIRST MAGIC NUMBER IN BRIDGE!

13

★ 13 CARDS IN EACH HAND
★ 13 CARDS IN EACH SUIT
★ 13 TRICKS IN THE DECK

BASICS OF THE GAME

Playing bridge is fun and learning the game should certainly be fun as well. Although the only way to learn the game is to be serious about it, let's approach the game with a relaxed attitude.

The first magic number in bridge is 13. There are 13 cards in each hand, 13 tricks in the deck and 13 cards in each suit. If you can count up to 13 in one suit, you're on the way to playing bridge. If you count to 13 in two suits, you're playing good bridge. If you count to 13 in all four suits, you're an expert.

PLAYERS

Bridge is played by four people. The players facing each other are partners. For convenience we will call one set of partners, North and South, the opposing partners, East and West.

DEAL

One person shuffles the cards, and *deals* the cards—starting to his left—clockwise, one at a time to each person including himself until all the cards are dealt out. Each person winds up with 13 cards.

SUITS

Each person then sorts his cards into suits—placing all the spades together, all the hearts together, all the clubs together and all the diamonds together. To avoid intermixing the suits, alternate the red and black suits in the hand. His *"hand"* may then look something like this:

CARD ORDER

SUITS & SYMBOLS
(IN THE ORDER OF RANK)

Ace
King
Queen
Jack
10
9
8
7
6
5
4
3
2

 Spades

 Hearts

 Diamonds

 Clubs

NOTE: *THE SUITS ARE IN ALPHABETICAL ORDER.*

CLUBS *ARE THE* **LOWEST**
SPADES *ARE THE* **HIGHEST**

HOW DO YOU WIN TRICKS

1. HIGH CARDS:

2. LONG SUITS:

3. TRUMPING:

EXAMPLE: HEARTS ARE TRUMP

The object of the game is to win *TRICKS*.

WHAT IS A TRICK?

After the bidding has ended and play commences, each player places a card on the table, face-up in turn clockwise until four cards are played. These four cards constitute a trick. As each player is required to follow suit, (that is, if the first card led is a diamond, each player must play a diamond if he has one) the highest card wins the trick.

Remember that this is a partnership game. Therefore, if partner's card is high enough to win the trick you do not have to waste a higher card on that trick.

The player who wins the trick then leads (makes the first play) to the next trick. If a player does not have a card in the suit led, he discards a card in another suit, or he may at his option, win the trick by *trumping it*—that is, playing any card in the trump suit.

WHAT IS TRUMP?

Trump is the suit selected in the bidding process by the partnership that wins the final contract. It could be either clubs, diamonds, hearts or spades.

Which brings us to the basic concepts of *Contract* bridge.

The object of the game is for a partnership to determine, by bidding, the trick-taking ability of the combined hands, and to arrive at a profitable contract.

If they are to play in a trump contract, they have to establish which of the suits they want to be the trump suit. A good trump suit is one in which the partnership has the majority of the cards, preferably eight or more cards in the combined hands.

They also have the option of playing in a no trump contract, where there isn't any trump suit.

The partnership arriving at the final contract is the declaring side. The person playing the hand is the declarer, his partner is "the dummy."

The opposing pair is called "the defenders."

BIDDING

Each hand is started by the dealer, who always makes the first call. He may either make a bid or a pass. The bidding proceeds to his left to the next player who likewise makes a bid or a pass. The process continues clockwise around the table.

(If all four players pass, the hand is thrown in and the deal passes on to the player on the left who deals a new hand). If one or more players make a bid, the bidding process continues until a bid is followed by three consecutive passes. That last bid is called the final contract.

Here is a typical example of the bidding process.

Assuming South is the dealer, this is how the bidding might proceed:

SOUTH	WEST	NORTH	EAST
1 ♡	1 ♠	2 ◇	pass
2 ♡	pass	4 ♡	pass
pass	pass		

The final contract is four hearts, requiring the winning of ten tricks with hearts as trumps. The declarer is South, because he was the first member of the partnership to bid hearts.

PLAY

The play is started by the defender to the left of the declarer, who places a card face-up on the table. This is called the opening lead. After the opening lead is made, the declarer's partner ("the dummy") places all his cards face-up on the table with the trump suit at his right. The declarer has the sole responsibility to play dummy's cards as well as his own.

This is what the table would look like after the opening lead:

14

The play continues trick by trick until all 13 tricks have been played. The declarer keeps all tricks won by his side neatly in front of him. The defenders' tricks are kept by one of the defenders, traditionally the partner of the defender who wins the first defensive trick. The tricks are placed alternately vertically and horizontally to make counting easier. At the end of the hand the table might look something like this:

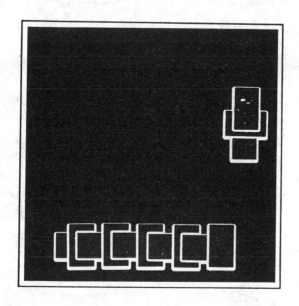

THE BIDDING LADDER

The higher ranking suits are spades and hearts. They are called the major suits. The lower ranking suits are diamonds and clubs, the minor suits. Ranking above them all is a category called, "No Trump."

You will note in the scoring table on page 18 that spades and hearts are worth 30 points per trick, while diamonds and clubs are worth only 20 points a trick. Therefore the *major* and *minor* suit designations. No trump (which is worth 40 points for the first trick and 30 points for each succeeding trick) ranks above them all.

THE BIDDING LADDER

BUT, NO TRUMP TOPS 'EM ALL!

HM!...
CLUBS,
DIAMONDS,
HEARTS,
SPADES.
THEY GO UP THE LINE IN ALPHABETICAL ORDER!

NO TRUMP

WE'RE THE MAJOR SUITS

WE'RE THE MINOR SUITS

I'M LOW MAN ON THE TOTEM POLE

H.L.

Therefore you can bid a new suit at the same level as long as it is a higher ranking suit. For example: you can bid one diamond over one club. But you cannot bid one club over one diamond. With a lower ranking suit you have to go to at least the next higher level to overcall. You would have to bid two clubs over one diamond.

Actually there can be as many as five bids on each level. The bidding can go, one club, one diamond, one heart, one spade, one no trump. But if the bidding were in the reverse order the minimum bidding would have to be one no trump, two spades, three hearts, four diamonds, five clubs.

In addition to bids in various levels of the four suits and no trump, there are only three other legal calls. 1. Pass, 2. Double (of an opponent's bid). 3. Redouble (of an opponent's double).

BOOK

The founding fathers of bridge developed the game quite logically.

With 13 tricks as the ultimate possibility, they established "Book" as six tricks (just under half of 13).

When you make a bid of one of a suit or no trump, you are obligating your partnership to win one trick above "Book" or seven tricks. A bid of two equals two tricks above book, or eight tricks, and so on until a bid of seven requires you to win *all 13 tricks*.

Therefore when you bid one spade, you are undertaking to win seven tricks with spades as the trump suit. Likewise, if you or your partner bids three no trump (for example) you are contracting to win nine tricks with no suit as trump.

OBJECT OF THE GAME

The object of the game is to win as many points as possible. You win points by bidding and fulfilling your contract. If you fail to make your contract there are penalties and the opponents win points (see chart pages 18-19). The main goal of the bidding is to arrive at the most profitable contract.

In order to accomplish this, it is necessary to evaluate the trick-taking ability of the combined partnership hands. As you can't show your hands to each other, you try to do so by informative bidding.

SCORING
BOOK = 6 TRICKS

TRICKS ABOVE BOOK BID AND MADE:

MAJOR SUITS	♠	SPADES:	**30** POINTS PER TRICK
	♥	HEARTS:	**30** POINTS PER TRICK
MINOR SUITS	♦	DIAMONDS:	**20** POINTS PER TRICK
	♣	CLUBS:	**20** POINTS PER TRICK

NO TRUMP: **40** POINTS, 1ST TRICK

30 POINTS, *EACH SUCCEEDING TRICK*

GAME = <u>100</u> POINTS

THEREFORE: GAME = 3NT, 4♠, 4♥, 5♦ OR 5♣ BID & MADE

PLUS BONUSES FOR BIDDING & MAKING GAME, SMALL SLAM & GRAND SLAM

RUBBER BRIDGE SCORING	BONUSES	
RUBBER	TWO-GAME **700** POINTS	THREE-GAME **500** POINTS
SLAMS	*VULNERABLE	NON-VUL.
SMALL SLAM	750	500
GRAND SLAM	1500	1000

*A RUBBER IS COMPLETED WHEN ONE SIDE HAS WON TWO GAMES. IF THE OPPONENTS HAVE WON ONE GAME IT IS A "THREE-GAME RUBBER", IF NOT IT'S "A TWO-GAME RUBBER."

*YOU ARE VULNERABLE WHEN YOUR SIDE HAS WON ONE GAME TOWARDS RUBBER, AND NON-VULNERABLE WHEN YOU HAVE NOT.

HONOR BONUSES ⟩ FOUR TRUMP HONORS IN ONE HAND = 100 POINTS. FIVE TRUMP HONORS (OR 4 ACES IN NT.) IN ONE HAND = 150 POINTS

PENALTIES
FOR NOT MAKING YOUR BID

	NOT VULNERABLE	VULNERABLE
UNDOUBLED	−50 POINTS PER TRICK	−100 POINTS PER TRICK
DOUBLED:	−100 FIRST TRICK −200 EACH ADD'L TRICK	−200 FIRST TRICK −300 EACH ADD'L TRICK
DOWN 1	−100 POINTS	−200 POINTS
DOWN 2	−300 POINTS	−500 POINTS
DOWN MORE	−200 POINTS FOR EACH ADD'L TRICK	−300 POINTS FOR EACH ADD'L TRICK

REDOUBLED = DOUBLE THE DOUBLED PENALTY.

HOWEVER,
IF YOU MAKE YOUR DOUBLED CONTRACT

YOU GET DOUBLE YOUR BID SCORE, *PLUS* 50 POINTS BONUS, *PLUS* 100 POINTS FOR EACH OVER-TRICK (NON-VUL.); 200 POINTS (VUL.).

MAKING A REDOUBLED CONTRACT GIVES YOU DOUBLE THE DOUBLED SCORE FOR TRICKS AND OVER-TRICKS.

The Dialogue of Bidding

WHAT IS THE

GOAL

PART SCORE
GAME
SLAM

OF BIDDING?

TO ARRIVE AT A <u>PROFITABLE</u> CONTRACT, BASED UPON THE _COMBINED ASSETS_ OF PARTNER'S HAND AND YOURS.

YOU HAVE TO DETERMINE THE _TRICK-TAKING ABILITY_ OF THE COMBINED HANDS!

HOW DO YOU EVALUATE YOUR HAND?

Actually you are trying to figure out the trick-taking ability of your cards.

To help simplify this procedure, Milton C. Work, many years ago, developed the *point count system*. Charles H. Goren, in more recent times, elaborated on it and popularized it to the extent that virtually everyone uses this "point count" system as the basis of their bidding.

Remember this: the point count system has nothing to do with the scoring of the game. It is merely an *artificial device* for evaluating your cards—but a very good one. If you just follow it mechanically you will do reasonably well. If you use it with insight and understanding you will do extremely well!

The basis of the point count is simple and easy to remember.

Mr. Work and Mr. Goren said, "Let's assign numerical values to the high cards in the deck." The most important card is the ace. They gave it a value of four points; the king is next, so it's worth three points; the queen is worth two points and the jack is worth one point.

Ace	=	4
King	=	3
Queen	=	2
Jack	=	1
		10 points

In each suit there are 10 points. As there are four suits, the entire deck has 40 points.

AVERAGE HAND

If you are neither the luckiest person on the block, nor the proverbial "hard luck" guy, you can expect to be dealt an average hand very often.

That's why we revolve our concepts on bidding around the *average hand*. By simple arithmetic, if there are 40 points in the entire deck, and there are four hands dealt, then an average hand contains *TEN POINTS*.

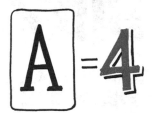 **= 4**

HOW MANY POINTS ARE THERE IN THE ENTIRE DECK?

40

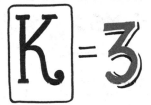 **= 3**

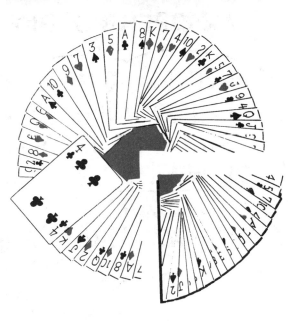

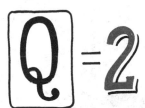 **= 2**

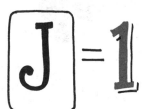 **= 1**

HOW MANY POINTS IN AN *AVERAGE HAND?*

10

WHAT IS AN OPENING BID?

(THE FIRST BID MADE (OTHER THAN THE CALL OF PASS) AFTER THE CARDS HAVE BEEN DEALT.)

AN OPENING BID SAYS:

PARTNER, I HAVE BETTER THAN AN AVERAGE HAND... AND I'M GIVING YOU AN IDEA OF WHERE MY STRENGTH LIES. *WHAT KIND OF HAND DO YOU HAVE?*

EXPERIENCE HAS SHOWN THAT A MINIMUM OF 13 POINTS IS NECESSARY FOR AN OPENING BID.

THE OPENING BID

As a bid of one (one heart, or one spade for example) obligates the partnership to win seven tricks—*or more than half* the possible number of 13 tricks—it is logical that to be the first player at the table to make a bid you should have *better* than an average hand.

Experience has shown that a minimum of 13 points in your hand is usually necessary to justify an opening bid.

THE OPENING BID OF ONE IN A SUIT

To determine whether you have an opening bid, here is how you count up your values.

1. *High Card Points.* First, simply add up the total points of all the high cards in your hand (four points for each ace, three points for each king, two points for each queen and one point for each jack).

2. *Distributional Points:*

In order to give value to the trick-taking ability of long suits, and, as a consequence, the trumping values of having short suits in a trump contract, points are added for having voids, singletons or doubletons.

These points are added to the high card points of the aces, kings, queens and jacks. If the combined total is 13 points you *may* make an opening bid of one in a suit. If the total is 14 points or more you *must* make an opening bid.

In counting distribution care must be exercised. Sometimes, the doubletons and singletons include honors. The evaluation has to be modified to take into consideration the trick-taking potential of the combination. The AK doubleton, for example, has the full two trick-taking ability as the AK, and it also has the value as a doubleton. So we assign it a total of eight points. At the other end of the scale, the Jx doubleton loses some of its value because the jack can be gobbled up by the A, K or Q and so it is assigned *only* its high card value of one point. In between the values are adjusted accordingly, as you will note in the chart on page 26.

POINT COUNT

HIGH CARDS }

A = **4** POINTS

K = **3** POINTS

Q = **2** POINTS

J = **1** POINT

DISTRIBUTIONAL POINTS FOR SUIT CONTRACTS:

Doubleton (2 cards in a suit) = **1** point

Singleton (1 card in a suit) = **2** points

Void (no cards in a suit) = **3** points

Doubletons with Honors		Singleton Honors	
AK=**8**	QJ=**3**	A.=**6**	Q.=**3**
AX=**5**	QX=**2**	K.=**4**	J.=**2**
KX=**4**	JX=**1**		

OKAY! I KNOW YOU NEED 13 POINTS TO OPEN THE BIDDING, BUT... WHICH SUIT DO I OPEN?...SUPPOSE I HAVE 2 SUITS OF EQUAL LENGTH?

THE ANSWER IS:

BE PREPARED! SELECT THE SUIT TO OPEN THAT MAKES YOUR REBID MOST CONVENIENT!

YOU MAY OPEN:

- **ANY SUIT** OF 5 OR MORE CARDS
- A **MINOR** SUIT OF 4 CARDS (♣ OR ♦)

> WITH NO 5-CARD MAJOR (♥ OR ♠) AND NO 4-CARD MINOR (♣ OR ♦)

- OPEN A **3-CARD** MINOR SUIT (♣ OR ♦) (WITH 3 CARDS IN BOTH MINORS, OPEN CLUBS)

- WITH 2 TOUCHING SUITS (OF EQUAL LENGTH) OPEN THE HIGHER, THEN REBID THE LOWER

- WITH 2 SUITS OF UNEQUAL LENGTH, BID THE **LONGER SUIT** FIRST

- WITH 2 5-CARD SUITS, OPEN THE HIGHER, THEN REBID THE LOWER*

*(EXCEPT WITH ♣ & ♠; OPEN CLUBS, THEN BID SPADES AND REBID SPADES.)

WHICH SUIT DOES THE OPENING BIDDER BID FIRST?

It is important to remember that a good trump suit is one in which you and your partner have the majority of the cards (preferably at least eight trumps between you). As most suit contracts that reach the game level are in the major suits (hearts or spades), the method we are learning is the so-called "five-card majors" system. This requires that you have at least five cards in a major suit to make an *opening bid* in it. It makes it possible for partner to support it with only three cards in the suit. The other suit bids possible are detailed in the chart on page 28.

Examples:

1. ♠ K 8 4
   ♡ A Q 10 8 3
   ◊ 6
   ♣ K Q 10 8

   Bid: 1 ♡

2. ♠ A K J 8 2
   ♡ Q J 9 8
   ◊ K 6
   ♣ 6 2

   Bid: 1 ♠

3. ♠ 9 2
   ♡ A K 3 2
   ◊ J 8 6
   ♣ A Q 10 3

   Bid: 1 ♣

4. ♠ 7 6 4 3
   ♡ A K 10 9
   ◊ A J 9
   ♣ Q 6

   Bid: 1 ◊

5. ♠ 8
   ♡ K J 3 2
   ◊ Q 10 9 8
   ♣ A K 7 3

   Bid: 1 ◊

6. ♠ Q 10 8 7 6
   ♡ A Q J 9 8
   ◊ A 4
   ♣ 9

   Bid: 1 ♠

GOALS

As there are substantial bonuses for bidding and making game and slam contracts, it is essential that the partnership, *as efficiently as possible*, determine their combined values.

If your partnership does not have sufficient values for game, you should try to find the most suitable contract at the lowest possible level.

If you *do* have enough values for game or slam, you should drive on to that level, determining your best suit or no trump as the final contract.

As a guide, the chart on the next page indicates the number of "points" the combined partnership *usually* needs to make a game or a slam.

HOW MUCH *COMBINED* STRENGTH DO YOU NEED TO REACH THE GOAL OF <u>GAME</u>?

<u>"USUALLY"</u>

3 NO TRUMP (9 TRICKS) = **26 POINTS**

4♠ OR 4♥ (10 TRICKS) = **26 POINTS**

5♣ OR 5♦ (11 TRICKS) = **29 POINTS**

<u>SLAMS</u>

SMALL SLAM (12 TRICKS) = **33 POINTS**

GRAND SLAM (13 TRICKS) = **37 POINTS**

THE SECOND MAGIC NUMBER:

26

THE NUMBER OF POINTS YOU AND YOUR PARTNER, COMBINED, NEED TO BID AND MAKE GAME IN A MAJOR SUIT OR NO TRUMP.

(90% OF ALL GAMES BID ARE IN ♥, ♠ OR NO TRUMP.)

THE MAGIC NUMBER: 26

Most games bid are in the major suits (hearts or spades) or in no trump. With 26 points as the minimum goal for game, it is wise for the partnership to determine "yea" or "nay" as quickly as possible.

It is here that we come to the key area of the bidding dialogue between partners, the response to an opening bid.

RESPONSES TO AN OPENING BID OF ONE IN A SUIT

When your partner has opened the bidding, you are the *responder*. You know your partner has at least 13 points, and he has mentioned a suit.

HOW DO YOU REACT?

With five points or less you simply pass! With six points or more you *must* find a bid.

There are some bids you can make that tell your complete story. If you have such a bid you should certainly make it. It makes life easier for your partner. He knows almost exactly what you have.

This type of bid is called a "limit bid." If you cannot make such a definitive bid, you make another appropriate bid and attempt to clarify it on your next turn to call.

THE MINIMUM RESPONSE
Six to Nine Points:*

These are high card points if you do not have support in your partner's suit. They include distributional points if you *do* have support.

1. With support in your partner's suit raise to two in his suit. (A limit bid)

2. With no support in his suit you may bid another suit at the *one* level.

3. When neither of these alternatives is possible bid one no trump. (A limit bid)

*In certain hands, when the honors are poorly placed, it can be as much as 10 points.

YOUR PARTNER'S JUST OPENED WITH 1 OF A SUIT... *HOW DO YOU REACT?*

WITH **6** TO **9** POINTS (OR A BAD **10**)
- RAISE PARTNER'S SUIT TO **2**.
- BID 1 IN A NEW SUIT.
- BID 1 NO TRUMP.

WHEW!! AT LEAST PARTNER HAS AN OPENING BID. *LET'S GO EASY!*

WITH **10** TO **12** POINTS
- BID 1 IN A NEW SUIT
- BID 2 IN A LOWER RANKING SUIT.

OH BOY!! THIS IS OUR HAND. WE MAY BE IN GAME COUNTRY. LETS FIND OUT IF AND WHERE!

WITH **13** TO **15** POINTS
- RAISE PARTNER'S SUIT TO **3**.
- BID 1 IN A NEW SUIT
- BID 2 IN LOWER RANKING SUIT.
- BID 2 N.T. WITH BALANCED HAND.

WOW! WE SHOULD HAVE A GAME... *AT LEAST!* LET'S DECIDE *WHERE!*

WITH **16** TO **18** POINTS (OR MORE)
- BID 1 IN A NEW SUIT
- BID 2 IN LOWER RANKING SUIT
- BID 3 N.T. WITH BALANCED HAND
- JUMP SHIFT WITH 17+ POINTS WITH FIT OR OWN STRONG SUIT.

YIPPEEE!! WE'RE IN SLAM TERRITORY. GAME IS "SURE." LET'S EXPLORE SLAM!

H.L.

Examples: Partner has opened the bidding with one heart. What do you bid with the following hands?

1. ♠ J 4	2. ♠ K Q 4 3	3. ♠ Q 5 2
♡ Q J 3	♡ J 4	♡ J 2
◊ K 6 5 4 3	◊ Q 5 2	◊ K Q 4 3
♣ Q 5 2	♣ 9 8 6 3	♣ 9 8 6 3
Bid: 2 ♡	Bid: 1 ♠	Bid: 1 NT

You will note that in hands one and three you have made *limit bids.*

In hand 1 your partner knows you have 6 to 9 points and support in his suit, no more, no less. Based on this information he will know what to do.

In hand 3 your partner knows you do *not* have good support in his suit and your hand is limited to 6 to 9 points. He should know what to do.

In hand 2, however, you have bid a new suit. Your hand can be as low as 6 points or many more (maybe as high as 17 points if you have not previously passed). Therefore this is an *unlimited* bid and will not be clarified until your next turn to bid.

10 to 12 points:

You have a right to be optimistic. You now know you're close to game if partner has slightly better than a minimum opening. The two calls you *cannot* make are one no trump or a raise to two in your partner's suit because they are bids *limited* to six to nine points. But you can make a bid of one in a higher ranking suit or a bid of two in a lower ranking suit. It is important to note at this point that to go to the *two level* in a new suit, *you need at least ten points.*

Examples: Partner has opened the bidding with one heart. What do you bid with the following hands?

1. ♠ Q 7 3 2	2. ♠ 8 6	3. ♠ J 9
♡ K Q 10 8	♡ K J 7	♡ Q 10 9 7
◊ 8 2	◊ 9 8 3	◊ A K J 10
♣ A 10 9	♣ A Q J 9 8	♣ 8 4 3
Bid: 1 ♠	Bid: 2 ♣	Bid: 2 ◊

13 to 15 points:

Here is where you know you want to reach at least game. You have at least 26 points between you. The only question is *where*.

With good support in your partner's suit, jump-raise to *three* in that suit.

Without very good support in your partners suit, but with a balanced hand, and stoppers in the other three suits, jump the bid to *two* no trump.

In all other cases, you can bid one of a higher ranking suit or two of a lower ranking suit. After partner bids again, you will be able to clarify your high card values and distribution.

16 or more points!

Here, game is virtually assured, and a real effort should be made to investigate the possibilities of slam.

With support in partner's suit you can make any forcing bid that is *unlimited* (you cannot jump-raise to three in that suit because that bid is limited to 13 to 15 points).

You can bid one of a higher ranking suit or two of a lower ranking suit.

If your hand is exceptionally strong — 17 points or better — you can "jump-shift." This means that you skip one level in a new suit.

Example: If partner opens the bidding with *one heart*, you may bid *two spades* or *three* clubs or *three* diamonds. These bids are considered jump-shifts.

Without good support in partner's suit, you may bid one of a higher ranking suit or two of a lowering ranking suit. With an exceptionally strong suit of your own and 18 or more points, you may *jump-shift* in your suit.

With a balanced hand of 16 to 18 points and stoppers in the other three suits, bid *three no trump*.

Let's take inventory at this point.

You have opened the bidding with a bid of one in a suit and your partner has responded. *The first phase* of the dialogue is now completed.

But where do we go from here?

REBIDS BY THE OPENING BIDDER

REBIDS BY THE OPENING BIDDER

In choosing your rebid you have to keep in mind the goals of bidding: part score, game, small slam or grand slam.

In response to your opening suit bid your partner has made either a *limit bid* or an *unlimited* bid.

If your partner has made a *limit bid*, your task is a little easier. You know within a narrow range partner's point count strength. You simply add partner's strength to yours and decide which of the bidding goals are probable, possible or unlikely. Then you rebid accordingly.

REBIDS AFTER PARTNER'S LIMIT BID RESPONSES

If partner's response was:

ONE NO TRUMP (6 to 9 points)

With a minimum hand up to 15 points, game is not likely. Therefore you want to settle into the *best possible part score* contract.

If your hand is reasonably balanced and suited to no trump play, simply pass.

If your hand is *unbalanced* you may (1) bid another *lower ranking* suit, giving your partner a choice of two suits, or (2) rebid your opening bid suit, if it is a good six card suit.

REBIDS by the OPENING BIDDER

1. WHEN RESPONDER HAS MADE A MINIMUM LIMIT BID

	YOU	PARTNER
	1 ♠	2 ♠ (6 to 9 POINTS)
OR	1 ♥	1 NT (6 to 9 POINTS)

IF YOU HOLD:

UP TO 15 POINTS
SETTLE FOR A PART SCORE

16 to 18 POINTS
INVITE GAME!

19 to 22 POINTS
GO FOR GAME!

37

♠ A Q J 8 2	♠ J	♠ 9
♡ K 7 5	♡ A Q J 7 6	♡ A K 10 7 6 3
◇ K 6 5	◇ K Q 9 6 4	◇ K 6 2
♣ 9 4	♣ 8 5	♣ K 8 4
You Ptnr.	You Ptnr.	You Ptnr.
1♠ 1 NT	1♡ 1 NT	1♡ 1 NT
Rebid: Pass	Rebid: 2 ◇	Rebid: 2 ♡

With a 16 + to 18 + point hand game is possible.

With a balanced hand raise to TWO NO TRUMP. (Partner can pass with a 6 or 7 point hand, or bid game with an 8 or 9 point hand.)

    With a good six card suit you may jump in your suit to the three level. (Partner can pass with a minimum. With a maximum, he may raise to game in your suit or no trump.)

Examples:

♠ A Q J 8 7	♠ 5	♠ K Q J 10 7 6
♡ K J 6	♡ A K 10 9 8 6	♡ A 6 2
◇ K Q 10	◇ A K 2	◇ A 8
♣ 7 6	♣ K 7 6	♣ Q 9
You Ptnr.	You Ptnr.	You Ptnr.
1♠ 1 NT	1♡ 1 NT	1♠ 1 NT
Rebid: 2 NT	Rebid: 3 ♡	Rebid: 3 ♠

With a 19 to 22 point hand game is likely.

Depending upon the character of your hand you may (1) raise to three no trump (2) jump to game in your suit, or (3) jump-shift in a new suit.

Examples:

♠ A Q 10 3 2	♠ A 5	♠ A Q J 9 6
♡ A Q 7	♡ A K J 10 7 6	♡ K Q 10 9
◇ K J 9	◇ K Q 8	◇ A 5 2
♣ A 10	♣ A 3	♣ A
You Ptnr.	You Ptnr.	You Ptnr.
1♠ 1 NT	1♡ 1 NT	1♠ 1 NT
Rebid: 3 NT	Rebid: 4 ♡	Rebid: 3 ♡

REBIDS AFTER PARTNER'S LIMIT BID RESPONSES (cont.)

If partner's response was:
A SINGLE RAISE IN YOUR SUIT (6 to 9 points)

Example:

You	Partner
1 ♠	2 ♠

With a minimum hand up to 15 points, simply pass.
With 16 to 18 points you may:
1. Raise suit to the three level, inviting partner to bid game with a maximum, or pass with a minimum.
2. Bid a new suit, asking partner to bid game with a maximum, or return to original suit at the lowest possible level with a minimum.

Examples:

♠ A J 10 4 3	♠ A K J 10 7	♠ A K 9 8 3
♡ K Q 2	♡ A 8 6	♡ K Q 10 6
◇ K 9 8	◇ A 5 2	◇ K J
♣ 8 3	♣ 8 5	♣ 8 2
You Ptnr.	You Ptnr.	You Ptnr.
1 ♠ 2 ♠	1 ♠ 2 ♠	1 ♠ 2 ♠
Rebid: Pass	Rebid: 3 ♠	Rebid: 3 ♡

When your original bid was a minor suit and the bidding has gone:

	You	Partner
	1 ♣	2 ♣
or	1 ◇	2 ◇

you may try to slide into a no trump game. Under those circumstances you may bid another suit, bid two no trump, or raise to three in the original suit. Again, partner with a minimum hand may pass the two no trump bid, bid two no trump over the second suit, return to three of the original suit or pass the three bid in the original suit. With a maximum hand partner may bid game or invite game.

Examples:

♠ K 8		♠ K Q 6		♠ Q J 7	
♡ A Q J 10		♡ K J 10 7		♡ A Q 9	
◇ A K 8 7 6		◇ 9		◇ 5	
♣ 10 9		♣ A K 9 8 6		♣ A Q J 10 3 2	
You	Ptnr.	You	Ptnr.	You	Ptnr.
1 ◇	2 ◇	1 ♣	2 ♣	1 ♣	2 ♣
Rebid: 2 NT		Rebid: 2 ♡		Rebid: 3 ♣	

With 19 to 22 points, a game contract is indicated. Here you, may jump directly to game, or make any *forcing bid* below game.

Examples:

♠ Q J 8		♠ A K 6		♠ A K 9 8 2	
♡ K Q 7 6		♡ A Q 7		♡ K 9	
◇ A K 10 7		◇ 6		◇ A Q 7 6	
♣ A 9		♣ A K 10 9 7 2		♣ K Q	
You	Ptnr.	You	Ptnr.	You	Ptnr.
1 ◇	2 ◇	1 ♣	2 ♣	1 ♠	2 ♠
Rebid: 3 NT		Rebid: 5 ♣ *		Rebid: 3 ◇	

A NOTE ON REEVALUATING YOUR HAND:

After partner has *supported* your suit, your distributional assets take on greater value. So, if you want to figure it strictly on a point-count basis, add one extra point for the fifth card in your suit and two points for each card over five.

IF PARTNER'S RESPONSE WAS A GAME-FORCE LIMIT BID:

(1.) A jump-raise in your suit.

Example:

You	Partner
1 ♡	3 ♡

*With an experienced partner an attempt can be made towards slam by either cue-bidding 2 ♡ or jumping in diamonds to indicate the singleton.

40

2. WHEN RESPONDER HAS MADE A GAME-FORCING LIMIT BID

EXAMPLES:	YOU	PARTNER
	1♥	3♥ (13 TO 15 POINTS)
OR	1♥	2 NT (13 TO 15 POINTS)
OR	1♥	3 NT (16 TO 18 POINTS)

THE KEY QUESTION IS:

DO WE SETTLE FOR GAME?   OR   DO WE TRY FOR SLAM?

or (2.) A jump in No Trump.

Examples:

	You	Partner
	1♡	2 NT
or	1♡	3 NT

The key question at this time is: Do we have just a game or is there a possibility for slam?

If slam does not seem likely, bid your game, giving the opponents as little information as possible.

Examples:

♠ 7	♠ A 8	♠ K 6 3
♡ K Q 10 6 2	♡ K J 9 6 4	♡ A K 8 6 4
◇ A 9 8 6	◇ A 9 2	◇ Q 9 2
♣ K J 5	♣ Q 8 7	♣ J 7
You Ptnr.	You Ptnr.	You Ptnr.
1♡ 3♡	1♡ 2 NT	1♡ 3 NT
Rebid: 4♡	Rebid: 3 NT	Rebid: Pass

If slam seems to be reasonably certain, and you know where you want to play it, just up and bid it if you have sufficient controls. Again, give as little information to the opponents as possible.

If slam is *likely,* or there is a question between a small or grand slam, you may have to make some "approach" bidding. This is to obtain additional information on which to make your decision.

Examples:

♠ A 5	♠ K Q	♠ A Q
♡ A K J 8 6	♡ A K J 7 6	♡ K Q 9 8 7 6
◇ A 7 4	◇ 9 8	◇ A 5
♣ K 10 2	♣ A J 10 5	♣ K Q 4
You Ptnr.	You Ptnr.	You Ptnr.
1♡ 3♡	1♡ 3♡	1♡ 3♡
Rebid: 6♡	Rebid: 4♣	Rebid: 4 NT*

Now let's consider what happens when responder has made an unlimited bid.

Examples:

	You	Partner		Partner has:
	1♡	1♠		6 to 17 or more points
or	1♡	2♣		10 to 17 or more points

The best thing you can do is to describe your hand as accurately as you can regarding its *strength* and *shape.*

---

*4 NT asks for aces (see Blackwood Convention).

3. WHEN RESPONDER HAS MADE AN UNLIMITED BID

EXAMPLES:		
	YOU	PARTNER
	1♥	1♠ (6 to 17 or more points)
OR	1♥	2♣ (10 to 17 or more points)

DESCRIBE YOUR HAND AS TO ITS
STRENGTH and SHAPE

HIGH CARD POINTS   DISTRIBUTION

Examples:

♠ J 8 7
♡ K Q 8 6
◇ A K 9 8
♣ J 5

You	Ptnr.
1◇	1♠

Rebid: 1 NT

♠ K J 9 8
♡ A 5
◇ K 7 6
♣ Q J 9 8

You	Ptnr.
1♣	1♡

Rebid: 1♠

♠ A K 7 6 5
♡ 7 6
◇ K Q 10 9
♣ K 3

You	Ptnr.
1♠	2♣

Rebid: 2◇

43

If you have described your hand accurately, the ball is now in your partner's corner. His next call should then clarify the type of hand he has. You should be able to carry on from there.

NO TRUMP BIDDING

Until now we have been concerned with opening bids in a suit and their responses. We now tackle a different kettle of fish — *no trump bidding*.

What is the major difference between a no trump and a trump contract?

In a trump contract when the opponents have length and strength in a side suit, you can prevent them from running that suit when you are out of it, by trumping it. Your *trumps* become the *stoppers*.

In a *no trump* contract that is not the case. It's desirable to have high cards in all the suits so the opponents cannot run a suit. These high card combinations are called *stoppers*. In order to have strength in all suits, you need a *balanced* hand.

As an opening one no trump bid automatically puts any response into at least the two level, the minimum point count requirement for an opening one no trump bid is higher than the minimum for an opening suit bid.

ONE NO TRUMP OPENING BID SHOWS 16 TO 18 HIGH CARD POINTS

There are *no points* counted for voids, singletons or doubletons. In a no trump contract, shortness in a suit is a *liability*, not an asset.

Therefore, an ideal one no trump opening bid is one in which you have a balanced hand (no singletons or voids), stoppers in at least three suits and 16 to 18 high card points.

The beauty of the one no trump bid is that it is a *limit* bid, 16 to 18 points. No more, no less. Partner knows within two points exactly what you have and can make his decision accordingly. *His responses are based upon this information.*

THE NO-TRUMP RACE!

NO TRUMP GOALS

GAME = 26 POINTS

SMALL 33 POINTS SLAM

37 POINTS GRAND SLAM

COMBINED PARTNERSHIP STRENGTH.

WHAT IS AN OPENING ONE NO TRUMP BID?

16 TO 18 High Card POINTS
WITH A "BALANCED" HAND,
AT LEAST 3 SUITS STOPPED!

WHAT IS A BALANCED HAND?

■ NO SINGLETONS OR VOIDS

■ THESE POSSIBLE DISTRIBUTIONS:

4,3,3,3   *5,3,3,2

4,4,3,2   *(5-CARD MINOR OR
            WEAK 5-CARD MAJOR)

■ AVOID WORTHLESS DOUBLETONS

WHAT IS A STOPPER?

■ A COMBINATION OF CARDS WHICH WILL "STOP" THE OPPONENTS FROM RUNNING A SUIT IF THEY WERE TO OPEN THAT SUIT.

EXAMPLES:

A	K	Q	J
X	X	J	10
		X	9
			X

Here are examples of typical one no trump opening bids:

1. ♠ Q J 8	2. ♠ A 3	3. ♠ A 7
♡ K J 4	♡ A K 8	♡ K Q 6
◇ A Q 7 6	◇ 9 6 3	◇ A J 8 6
♣ K 4 3	♣ A Q 7 3 2	♣ K J 3 2
16 H.C. Points	17 H.C. Points	18 H.C. Points

Now, here are some hands that may *look* like one no trump opening bids, but they are *not*. They have some elements of the no trump bid, but not *all*.

4. ♠ A	5. ♠ A 7 6	6. ♠ A Q 8 6 4
♡ K Q 9 3	♡ K J 7 4	♡ A K
◇ A 10 8 6	◇ Q 10 2	◇ K 10 6 3
♣ K J 10 7	♣ K J 9	♣ 7 2
Bid: 1 ◇	Bid: 1 ♣	Bid: 1 ♠

Hand 4 has 17 high card points, but it is *unbalanced*, containing a singleton. In a suit contract the hand is worth 19 points including distribution.

Hand 5 has the proper *distribution*, but contains only 14 points—not enough for the one no trump opening bid.

Hand 6 has 16 high card points, enough for a one no trump opener, but it has a number of drawbacks which make a suit opening bid superior. First, it has a good five-card *major* suit. Secondly, it contains two doubletons, one of which, the club holding, is a worthless doubleton. In a suit contract the hand is worth 18 points.

RESPONSES TO AN OPENING ONE NO TRUMP BID WITH A BALANCED HAND

This is where the magic number 26 comes in very handy. You know your partner has 16 to 18 high card points. You simply add *your* high card points to your partner's known points. If they add up to 26 points, just up and bid "three no trump"—game. For example, you have ten high card points. You add it to the "16" you know your partner has. It totals 26 so you bid three no trump. I call this a *"drop dead"* bid. Your partner must pass. You know his hand and you have made the final decision.

But suppose you have only *seven* high card points. You add that to 16 points. It totals 23 points—not enough for game. Even if partner has 18 points there is still not enough

RESPONSES TO PARTNER'S OPENING 1 NO TRUMP BID

"I'VE GOT 16 TO 18 HIGH CARD POINTS. WHAT DO YOU SAY, PARTNER?" 1 N.T.

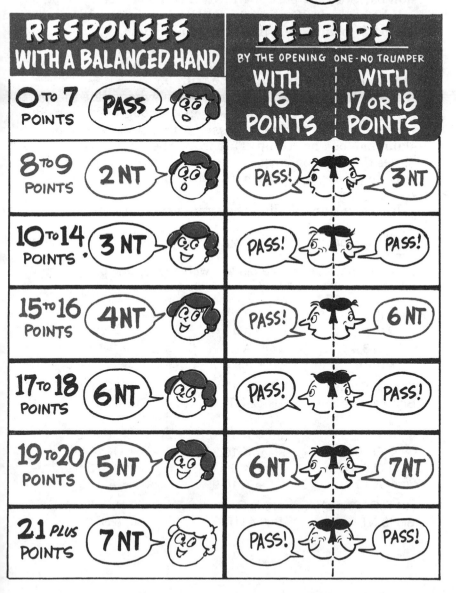

RESPONSES WITH A BALANCED HAND		RE-BIDS BY THE OPENING ONE-NO TRUMPER	
		WITH 16 POINTS	WITH 17 OR 18 POINTS
0 TO 7 POINTS	PASS		
8 TO 9 POINTS	2 NT	PASS!	3 NT
10 TO 14 POINTS	3 NT	PASS!	PASS!
15 TO 16 POINTS	4 NT	PASS!	6 NT
17 TO 18 POINTS	6 NT	PASS!	PASS!
19 TO 20 POINTS	5 NT	6 NT	7 NT
21 PLUS POINTS	7 NT	PASS!	PASS!

for game. Therefore, with seven points or *less* you usually *pass* your partner's opening one no trump bid.

Sometimes you have eight or nine points. You add that to partner's minimum of 16 points and it's not enough for game. You add them to partner's *possible* 18 points and it *is* enough for game. Now, what do you do?

You simply bid *two* no trump; and throw the final decision back to your partner. I call this a *"ping-pong"* bid.

If he has only 16 points he will pass. If he has 18 points or a good 17 points, he will bid *three* no trump.

Similarly, slam bidding over an opening one no trump uses the same principles. If your points added to partner's "16" total 33 points, bid six no trump.

If you have 15 to 16 points (which when added to partner's minimum of 16 points is not enough for slam, but when added to partner's *possible* 18 points *is* enough for slam) bid *four* no trump. This is another "ping-pong" bid. It tosses the decision back to partner. It says to partner, "With only 16 points, *pass*. With 18 points or a good 17 points, bid *six no trump.*"

In grand slam bidding the same principles apply.

Example responses to opening one no trump bids with balanced hands:

Partner has opened the bidding with one no trump. What do you respond with these hands?

1. ♠ Q 4 3	2. ♠ K 6 2	3. ♠ 7 6
♡ K 7 6 2	♡ 8 4 3	♡ K Q 4
◇ Q 8 4	◇ A 6 3	◇ 9 7 6
♣ 9 7 6	♣ J 9 8 7	♣ A J 6 4 3
(7 H.C. Points)	(8 H.C. Points)	(10 H.C. Points)
Bid: Pass	Bid: 2 NT	Bid: 3 NT

4. ♠ A J 9	5. ♠ A J 10	6. ♠ A J 10
♡ Q 10 3	♡ K 10 3	♡ K 10 3
◇ Q 6 5 3	◇ K 6 5 3	◇ K J 9 8
♣ A J 7	♣ A 10 9	♣ A J 10
(14 H.C. Points)	(15 H.C. Points)	(17 H.C. Points)
Bid: 3 NT	Bid: 4 NT	Bid: 6 NT

50

RESPONSES TO AN OPENING ONE NO TRUMP BID WITH AN UNBALANCED HAND

With an unbalanced hand, a suit contract is often more desirable than a no trump contract. It may produce more tricks because of the ruffing values in the hand. Your trumps act as a stopper to prevent the opponents from running any long suit they may have. Whereas, with a balanced hand containing seven or less points you should pass, with an unbalanced hand you may bid a suit which contains five or more cards, even with *much less* than seven points.

For example:

♠ 9 5 2
♡ 6
♢ Q 9 7 6 5 4
♣ 7 6 2

With this hand you would bid two diamonds over partner's opening one no trump bid. At a no trump contract your hand might produce no tricks at all, unless partner had specifically ♢ AKx. In a diamond contract, you should produce at least four tricks. You know partner has no less than two diamonds, with possibly an honor. That gives you a minimum of an eight-card trump suit. While you easily might be set in a one no trump contract, your prospects for making two diamonds are quite good.

Let's look at these two possibilities:

Your Hand:	*Partner's Hand:*	
♠ 9 5 2	**A.** ♠ A K 3	**B.** ♠ J 10
♡ 6	♡ K Q 7 4	♡ K Q 7 4
♢ Q 9 7 6 5 4	♢ J 10	♢ A K 3
♣ 7 6 2	♣ Q J 10 5	♣ Q J 10 5

In *Hand A*, one no trump will probably go down one or two tricks while two diamonds will probably make eight tricks. In *Hand B*, the optimum of what you could expect from your partner in the diamond suit, the opponents will make a *minimum* of seven tricks in no trump (four spades, two clubs and one heart) for down one, while a two diamond contract would probably be successful.

RESPONSES
TO PARTNER'S OPENING 1NT BID WITH UNBALANCED HANDS

WITH 5 CARDS OR LONGER SUIT,

WITH **0** TO **7** POINTS

> I BID **2** OF MY SUIT*
>
> * EXCEPT CLUBS

WITH **8** TO **14** POINTS

EXPLORE FOR GAME OR BID GAME DIRECTLY

> WITH MINOR SUITS I TEND TO BID 2 N.T. WITH 8 POINTS, AND 3 N.T. WITH 9 POINTS OR MORE.

> WITH 1 OR 2 MAJOR SUITS, I CAN BID 2♣ STAYMAN.

> WITH 9 OR MORE POINTS I CAN BID 3♥ OR 3♠. WITH A 6 CARD MAJOR, I CAN BID 4♥ OR 4♠

WITH **15** POINTS OR MORE EXPLORE FOR SLAM

> I CAN JUMP TO 3 IN MY SUIT; USE STAYMAN, CHECK FOR ACES VIA CUE BIDS, GERBER.

Therefore, with an unbalanced hand containing zero to seven points, you may bid 2 ◇, 2 ♡, or 2 ♠ in response to partner's opening one no trump bid (2 ♣ is reserved for a specialized Stayman bid, which we will discuss shortly).

With 10 to 14 points with a five-card major suit you may jump to three in the major suit. With a six-card major and nine or more points you can bid game (4 ♡ or 4 ♠).

Examples:

1. ♠ A K 9 6 2	2. ♠ K 4 3	3. ♠ A K 10 9 7 6
♡ 7 6	♡ A Q J 8 3	♡ 4
◇ Q J 9 8	◇ 3 2	◇ Q 9 8 4
♣ 9 3	♣ K 7 3	♣ 6 2
Bid: 3 ♠	Bid: 3 ♡	Bid: 4 ♠

With 10 to 14 points with a five-card minor suit tend to bid three no trump. However, if the hand is unbalanced, or if you have a six-card suit, you may jump to three in the minor suit, when there is a possibility of a slam in a suit contract.

Examples:

1. ♠ 8 7	2. ♠ J 6	3. ♠ 9 8 6
♡ K J 3	♡ A 7	♡ K 7 3
◇ A Q 10 8 7	◇ K Q 3	◇ A
♣ 7 6 3	♣ Q J 10 6 3 2	♣ A K J 10 8 3
Bid: 3 NT	Bid: 3 NT	Bid: 3 ♣

Hands 1 and 2 will have a better chance of making game for the partnership in no trump, rather than in an eleven-trick minor suit contract.

Hand 3, however, has chances for a minor suit small slam and an indication of that fact can be made by bidding three clubs.

With eight to nine points and a five-card minor suit, bid two no trump.

Examples:

1. ♠ 9 7 2	2. ♠ 9 6	3. ♠ Q 7 6
♡ 7 6	♡ J 6 3	♡ J
◇ A J 8 7 6	◇ Q 8 7	◇ Q J 9 6 3
♣ K 8 7	♣ A Q 8 6 3	♣ Q J 7 2
Bid: 2 NT	Bid: 2 NT	Bid: 2 NT

You will note that in *Hand 3,* although your hand is unbalanced, you should bid two no trump.

STAYMAN CONVENTION

TO TRY TO FIND A FOUR/FOUR FIT IN A MAJOR SUIT, AND HAVE THE OPENING NO TRUMP BIDDER PLAY IT.

1 N.T. "I HAVE A BALANCED HAND WITH 16 TO 18 HIGH CARD POINTS"

STAYMAN: "I HAVE 8 OR MORE HIGH CARD POINTS WITH ONE OR TWO MAJOR SUITS...

DO YOU HAVE A FOUR-CARD MAJOR SUIT?"

ANSWERS TO STAYMAN:

2♦ "SORRY, I HAVE NEITHER FOUR HEARTS NOR FOUR SPADES!"

2♥ "I HAVE FOUR HEARTS. I DO NOT HAVE FOUR SPADES"

2♠ "I HAVE FOUR SPADES... BUT I MAY ALSO HAVE FOUR HEARTS!"

With major suits of four or more cards and at least eight points, you have an additional tool, the Stayman two-club convention.

THE STAYMAN CONVENTION

The purpose of the Stayman convention is to find an "eight-card major suit fit" and have the opening no trump bidder become the declarer. Many times you can make four hearts or four spades, if the hand is even slightly unbalanced, while the partnership will go down in three no trump.

It is often wise to have the opening no trump bidder play the hand. He usually has high card combinations such as AQ, AKJ, KJ10, AJ10, Kx which will produce an extra trick if his hand is led up to. These are called "tenace" positions.

Follow the accompanying chart on page 54 for the Stayman dialogue.

Here are typical hands where you can use Stayman:

Your partner has opened one no trump. What do you bid with:

1. ♠ Q J 8 6
   ♡ J 10 7 3
   ◇ A 4 2
   ♣ 7 2

   Bid: 2 ♣

2. ♠ Q 10 9 7 6
   ♡ A 8 4 3
   ◇ K 9
   ♣ 6 3

   Bid: 2 ♣

3. ♠ Q J 6 3
   ♡ K 10 6
   ◇ A 7 6 4
   ♣ 8 2

   Bid: 2 ♣

4. ♠ 6 3
   ♡ K J 10 6 5
   ◇ 8 5
   ♣ A J 7 5

   Bid: 2 ♣

5. ♠ 6 3
   ♡ K J 10 6 5
   ◇ 8 5
   ♣ J 7 5 3

   Bid: 2 ♡

6. ♠ Q J 6 3
   ♡ K 10 6 2
   ◇ 7 6 4
   ♣ 8 2

   Bid: Pass

Hands 1, 2, 3 and 4 are perfect hands for a 2 ♣ Stayman response. *Hand 5,* although similar to *Hand 4,* contains only five points and is therefore too weak for a Stayman bid. *Hand 6,* while it has the perfect *shape* for a Stayman bid, contains only six points and should be passed.

CONTINUING THE STAYMAN DIALOGUE

In answer to your 2 ♣ Stayman bid, your partner can make only three bids: (1) two diamonds; (2) two hearts; (3) two spades. Based upon the response you make your decision.

1. If the response is two diamonds showing no four-card major, here are your alternatives:

If you have no five-card major: With eight to nine points, bid two no trump. With 10 to 14 points bid three no trump.

Examples:

Partner had opened 1 NT. You then bid 2 ♣, Stayman, to which partner responded 2 ◊. What do you do now?

1. ♠ K 10 9 6	2. ♠ Q 9 8 6	3. ♠ Q J 6 3
♡ Q 10 8 3	♡ A 8 4 3	♡ K 10 6
◊ K 7 6	◊ K 9	◊ A 7 6 4
♣ 7 2	♣ 6 3 2	♣ 8 2
Bid: 2 NT	Bid: 2 NT	Bid: 3 NT

If you have a five-card major:

With eight to nine points bid your five-card major at the two level.

With 10 or more points bid your five-card major at the *three* level.

Examples:

4. ♠ Q J 6 5 3	5. ♠ 8 2	6. ♠ A Q 10 7 3
♡ K Q 6 2	♡ A J 9 8 5	♡ K 6 3
◊ 6 2	◊ K J 7 5	◊ 8 3
♣ 8 3	♣ 6 3	♣ J 8 7
Bid: 2 ♠	Bid: 2 ♡	Bid: 3 ♠

2. If the response is two hearts, showing at least four hearts, here are your alternatives:

If hearts is your suit, raise to three hearts with eight points; raise to four hearts with 9 to 14 points.

If hearts is not your suit, and you have only four spades, bid two no trump with eight to nine points; bid three no trump with 10 to 14 points.

If hearts is not your suit, and you have *five* spades, bid two spades with eight to nine points; bid *three* spades with 10 or more points.

Examples:

1. ♠ Q 9 3 2	2. ♠ K 9 3 2	3. ♠ K J 10 3
♡ A J 8 3	♡ A Q 8 3	♡ 9 3
◊ J 10 8	◊ 9 2	◊ K 9 6
♣ 9 7	♣ J 10 8	♣ J 10 3 2
Bid: 3 ♡	Bid: 4 ♡	Bid: 2 NT

4. ♠ K Q 10 3
    ♡ 9 3
    ◇ K 9 6
    ♣ Q 10 3 2
Bid: 3 NT

5. ♠ K J 10 6 3
    ♡ 9 3
    ◇ K 9
    ♣ J 10 3 2
Bid: 2 ♠

6. ♠ K J 10 6 3
    ♡ A 3
    ◇ K 9
    ♣ 10 9 3 2
Bid: 3 ♠

3. If the response is two spades, showing at least four spades (and *possibly* four hearts) here are your alternatives:

If spades is your suit, raise to three spades with 8 points; raise to four spades with 9 to 14 points.

Examples:

1. ♠ K J 8 7
    ♡ 10 9 6 3
    ◇ K 6 4
    ♣ J 9
Bid: 3 ♠

2. ♠ K J 8 7
    ♡ Q 10 6 3
    ◇ K 6 2
    ♣ 7 6
Bid: 4 ♠

3. ♠ K Q 9 8 3
    ♡ Q J 4
    ◇ K J 3
    ♣ 3 2
Bid: 4 ♠

If spades is not your suit, and you have only four hearts bid two no trump with eight to nine points; bid three no trump with 10 to 14 points.

Examples:

1. ♠ Q J 4
    ♡ K 10 9 3
    ◇ Q 6 5 3
    ♣ 7 4
Bid: 2 NT

2. ♠ Q J 4
    ♡ K Q 10 9
    ◇ Q 6 5 3
    ♣ 7 4
Bid: 3 NT

3. ♠ K J 4
    ♡ K J 9 8
    ◇ 6 3
    ♣ K Q 6 2
Bid: 3 NT

If spades is not your suit, and you have five hearts, bid two no trump with 8 to 9 points; bid three hearts with 10 to 14 points.

Examples:

1. ♠ K 4 3
    ♡ Q J 9 8 2
    ◇ Q 6 2
    ♣ 5 3
Bid: 2 NT

2. ♠ 5 3
    ♡ Q J 9 8 2
    ◇ K J 6
    ♣ K 4 3
Bid: 3 ♡

3. ♠ K 4 2
    ♡ K Q 10 9 4
    ◇ K Q 4
    ♣ 8 3
Bid: 3 ♡

THE DIALOGUE NOW SHIFTS BACK TO THE OPENING ONE NO TRUMP BIDDER

If the responder's bid was at the *two* level, the opening bidder, with 16 points, passes the two no trump bid; passes the two hearts or two spades bids with three card support in the suit; or converts the suit bid to two no trump with only two cards in partner's suit.

Examples: You are the opening one no trump bidder and you hold:

1. ♠ K J 6	2. ♠ Q J	3. ♠ K 4 3
♡ Q 3	♡ K 10 3	♡ A 6 2
◇ A K 7 3	◇ A J 8 7	◇ K J 8 7
♣ K 9 8 2	♣ K Q 6 3	♣ A J 8

The bidding had proceeded: You had bid one no trump; partner responded two clubs, to which you answered two diamonds. What do you say now, if partner's next bid is:
(A) 2 NT.
 In all three hands, with only 16 points, you simply pass.
(B) 2 ♡.
 In Hand 1, you bid 2 NT. *In Hands 2 and 3* with three-card heart support you pass.
(C) 2 ♠
 In Hands 1 and 3, with three card spade support you pass. In *Hand 2* with only two spades you bid 2 NT.

With a good 17 point or an 18 point hand the opening bidder raises to three no trump, or with support in partner's bid suit raises the suit to the four-level.

Examples:

4. ♠ K J 9	5. ♠ A 9	6. ♠ Q J 10
♡ A Q 3	♡ K 9 3	♡ A 3
◇ A J 9 3	◇ A Q 10 6	◇ A K 8 6
♣ K 6 2	♣ A 10 9 8	♣ K J 9 7

In the continuing Stayman dialogue, after an opening one no trump by you, two clubs, Stayman, by partner, two diamonds by you, what do you bid with the above hands after partner bids:
(A) 2 NT.
 In all three hands, with 18 points or a good 17 points, you bid 3 NT.
(B) 2 ♡
 In *Hands 4 and 5,* with three card support in hearts, bid 4 ♡. In *hand 6,* bid 3 NT.

(C) 2 ♠

    In *Hands 4 and 6,* with three card support in Spades, bid 4 ♠.
    In *Hand 5* bid 3 NT.

If responder's bid was a new suit at the three level, opening bidder raises suit bid to four with three-card support or bids three no trump with only two cards in the suit.

Examples:

1.	♠ A Q	2.	♠ K J 10	3.	♠ Q J 10
	♡ K J 9		♡ A 3		♡ K 9 3
	◇ K 9 6 3		◇ A Q 9 7 6		◇ A 10
	♣ Q J 8 4		♣ K 9 3		♣ K Q J 9 3

Hand 1. Bid 4 ♡ over partner's 3 ♡; 3 NT over partner's 3 ♠.
Hand 2. Bid 3 NT over partner's 3 ♡; 4 ♠ over partner's 3 ♠.
Hand 3. Bid 4 ♡ over partner's 3 ♡; 4 ♠ over partner's 3 ♠.

If responder's bid was a raise to three of opener's major suit bid, opener passes with 16 points but raises to four in the suit with 17 or 18 points.

Examples:

1.	♠ K J 9 8	2.	♠ K 9	3.	♠ A Q 9 3
	♡ A 6 3		♡ Q J 10 6		♡ K J 9 2
	◇ Q J 6		◇ A K 7 6		◇ A J 3
	♣ K Q 9		♣ K J 3		♣ K 4

Hand 1. Pass over partner's 3 ♠ bid.
Hand 2. Bid 4 ♡ over partner's 3 ♡ bid.
Hand 3. Bid 4 ♠ over partner's 3 ♠ bid. Bid 4 ♡ over partner's 3 ♡ bid.

Finally, if the opening no trump bidder had bid two spades in response to Stayman, and *ALSO* has a four-card heart suit, he can correct a two no trump or three no trump responder's bid to three or four hearts.

Examples:

A Stayman dialogue has gone:

(A)	You	Partner	**or (B)**	You	Partner
	1 NT	2 ♣		1 NT	2 ♣
	2 ♠	2 NT		2 ♠	3 NT

Although partner has denied having a spade suit, you *know* he has a heart suit—because he would not have started the Stayman sequence without at least *one* major suit. What do you bid, therefore, with these hands?

1. ♠ A Q 7 6
    ♡ K J 8 4
    ◇ K J 6
    ♣ Q 3

2. ♠ K J 8 4
    ♡ A Q 7 6
    ◇ K J 6
    ♣ K 3

3. ♠ K J 9 2
    ♡ A J 10 3
    ◇ K Q 9
    ♣ A 3

(A) Bid: 3 ♡
(B) Bid: 4 ♡

(A) Bid: 4 ♡
(B) Bid: 4 ♡

(A) Bid: 4 ♡
(B): Bid: 4 ♡

STAYMAN INTERFERENCE

Sometimes you would like to bid Stayman over your partner's opening one no trump bid, but the opponents have interfered by overcalling. How do you handle this situation? Suppose the bidding has gone:

partner	opponent	you
1 NT	2 ♣	?

You indicate your Stayman bid by cue-bidding the opponent's suit. In this case you would bid *three clubs*. Your partner would then respond in the same manner as if you had bid two clubs, Stayman. However, you would be one level higher, so his responses would be, "three diamonds" (no four-card major), "three hearts", (with four or more hearts) or "three spades" (with four or more spades).

Examples:

Over partner's opening 1 NT bid, opponents bid 2 ♣. What do you bid with:

1. ♠ A J 9 6
    ♡ Q 10 9 6
    ◇ 10 9 3
    ♣ Q 3
Bid: 3 ♣

2. ♠ A 6 4 2
    ♡ Q 8 5 2
    ◇ J 3
    ♣ 10 8 3
Bid: Pass

3. ♠ K Q 10 9 3
    ♡ 10 6 3
    ◇ J 9 2
    ♣ 6 3
Bid: 2 ♠

Hand 1. has just enough to bid Stayman. *Hand 2.* is too weak. *Hand 3.* is just about fine for competing with a non-forcing spade bid.

Over partner's opening 1 NT bid, opponents bid 2 ◇. What do you bid with:

WHAT HAPPENS WHEN YOU WANT TO BID STAYMAN AND THE OPPONENT OVERCALLS?

EVERYBODY WANTS T' GET INTO DA' ACT!

STAYMAN
OVER OPPONENT'S INTERFERENCE

PARTNER	OPPONENT	YOU	STAYMAN
1NT	2♦	?	= 3♦
1NT	2♣	?	= 3♣

STAYMAN = CUE BID IN OPPN'T'S SUIT

ANY OTHER SUIT BID AT **LOWEST POSSIBLE LEVEL** IS *NON-FORCING.* YOU HAVE TO *JUMP* IN ANOTHER SUIT TO BE *FORCING!*

ON WHAT TYPE HANDS CAN YOU USE STAYMAN OVER OPPONENT'S INTERFERENCE?

1. YOUR HAND SHOULD BE **9** POINTS OR BETTER.
2. YOU CAN HANDLE ANY REPLY PARTNER MAKES.
3. *REMEMBER!* OVER OPPONENT'S 2♣ OVERCALL YOU HAVE GREATER LEEWAY THAN OVER 2♦ OVERCALL.

61

4. ♠ A 10 9 6	5. ♠ A J 9 3	6. ♠ K 8 3
♡ Q 10 9 6	♡ Q 9 8 7	♡ A Q J 6 3
◇ A 3	◇ 8 7 3	◇ 10 9
♣ 6 3 2	♣ 5 2	♣ 9 8 3
Bid: 3 ◇	Bid: Pass	Bid: 3 ♡

Hand 4. is strong enough for Stayman. *Hand 5* is too weak.
Hand 6. requires a jump bid to indicate a good five-card major suit and game-going strength.

FORCING BIDS

When is a bid forcing, (partner *must* bid again) or when is it not forcing (partner *may* pass) is one of the most important concepts of partnership bidding.

To comprehend this fully, two other aspects of bidding should be understood. The *limit bid* and the *unlimited* bid.

A *limit bid* is one that tells partner (within a range of two or three points) the strength of the hand. For example, we know that an opening *one no trump* bid is 16 to 18 points. That is a limit bid.

We also know that a *response* of one no trump to an opening diamond, heart or spade bid is six to nine points. That is a *limit bid*.

If you raise partner's opening suit bid from one to two, it is also a *limit* bid, showing six to nine points.

As a general rule, most limit bids are *non-forcing*. You know within two or three points what partner has, and you can make your decision accordingly, whether to pass or to bid on.

The exceptions are jump bids by responders who have never previously passed, such as:

opener	responder
1 ♠	3 ♠ = 13 to 15 points
1 ♠	2 NT = 13 to 15 points

These bids are forcing to game.

Unlimited bids by responders are *forcing*.

Suppose you are dealer and you open the bidding with one heart and your partner responds one spade. He can have as little as six points or as many as 17 or more. His bid is *unlimited* and therefore *forcing*.

It follows that any new suit bid by a responder, who

WHEN IS A BID *FORCING*?

OPENER, YOU *MUST* BID AGAIN, IF:
■ UN-PASSED PARTNER BIDS A NEW SUIT.
■ UN-PASSED PARTNER MAKES A JUMP BID BELOW GAME.

OPENER, YOU *MAY* PASS, IF:
■ PARTNER RAISES YOUR SUIT ONE LEVEL.
■ PARTNER BIDS 1 OR 3 NO TRUMP.
■ PARTNER IS A PREVIOUSLY PASSED HAND.

RESPONDER, YOU *MUST* BID, IF:
■ OPENER BIDS 2 IN A SUIT AS AN OPENING BID.
■ OPENER MAKES A REVERSE BID.
■ OPENER MAKES A JUMP SHIFT.
■ OPENER BIDS A NEW SUIT AFTER YOU HAD
   PREVIOUSLY RAISED HIS ORIGINAL SUIT.

has never previously passed, is *unlimited* and therefore *forcing*.

You have probably noticed that we referred to a "responder who *has never previously passed.*" Once a player has originally passed, his hand is *limited*. We *know* he has less than 14 points.

The accompanying chart covers most of the possible forcing and non-forcing bids. See if you can figure out which bids are *limited* and which are *unlimited*.

Examples:

Which of these bids are forcing? Which are non-forcing?

SOUTH	WEST	NORTH	EAST
1. 1 ♦	Pass	1 ♠	Pass

Is North's 1 ♠ bid forcing?

2. Pass	Pass	1 ♦	Pass
1 ♠	Pass		

Is South's 1 ♠ bid forcing?

3. 1 ♠	Pass	1 NT	Pass

Is North's 1 NT bid forcing?

SOUTH	WEST	NORTH	EAST
4. Pass	1 ♠	Pass	2 ♣
Pass	2 ♦	Pass	2 ♡
Pass			

Is East 2 ♡ bid forcing?

5. 1 ♠	Pass	3 ♠	Pass

Is North's 3 ♠ bid forcing?

6. 1 NT	Pass	3 NT	Pass

Is North's 3 NT bid forcing?

1. North's 1 ♠ bid is forcing. It is a new suit by a responder who has never previously passed.

2. South's 1 ♠ bid is non-forcing. South had previously passed.

3. North's 1 NT bid is non-forcing. It is a limit bid—6 to 9 points.

4. East's 2 ♡ is forcing. It is a new suit by a responder who has never previously passed.

5. North's 3 ♠ bid is forcing to game.

6. North's 3 NT bid is non-forcing. Game has been reached.

COMPETITION

Life would be very easy if there were no competition, but it would most likely be very dull as well. Up to now we've been bidding, mostly without interference, just between partner and ourselves. But sometimes, the opponents get into the bidding, and it bollixes things up a bit. It makes life difficult for us. They may even steal the bid from us.

Well, if they can make things difficult for us, we can make things tough for them when *they* open the bidding.

We can compete.

THE GREAT AMERICAN TRADITION!
COMPETITION

> SURE! YOUR SIDE OPENED THE BIDDING, *BUT!*...

REASONS FOR COMPETING!

> **1.** WE CAN <u>OUT-BID</u> YOU TO A PART SCORE OR GAME!

> **2.** MY PARTNER WILL KNOW WHAT TO <u>LEAD</u>, IF YOU <u>DO</u> GET THE CONTRACT!

> **3.** WE'LL PUSH YOU UP <u>TOO HIGH</u> AND *BEAT YOU!*

> **4.** WE'LL <u>SCARE</u> YOU INTO NOT BIDDING ENOUGH!

WAYS OF COMPETING
OVER OPPONENTS' OPENING SUIT BID

1. SIMPLE OVERCALL = GOOD SUIT, "CLOSE TO" AN OPENING BID. [AT TWO-LEVEL IT HAS TO BE STRONGER]

2. JUMP OVERCALL = VERY GOOD HAND, VERY GOOD SUIT. [BUT IT IS NOT FORCING]

3. NO TRUMP OVERCALL = 16 TO 18 POINTS WITH GOOD CONTROLS IN OPPONENT'S SUIT.

4. TAKE-OUT DOUBLE = OPENING BID OR BETTER, SUPPORT FOR ALL UN-BID SUITS; OR OWN INDEPENDENT SUIT WITH 18 OR MORE POINTS. [PARTNER IS ASKED TO BID BEST SUIT.]

5. CUE-BID (IN OPPONENT'S SUIT) = *POWERHOUSE HAND!* GAME-FORCING BID, EQUAL TO OPENING TWO-BID; PARTNER MAY NOT PASS SHORT OF GAME.

6. PRE-EMPTIVE OVERCALLS (DOUBLE JUMP OR MORE) = 7 OR MORE CARDS IN SUIT. [LESS THAN OPENING BID HIGH CARD STRENGTH.]

7. "UNUSUAL" NO TRUMP (JUMP BID TO 2 NO TRUMP) = OVER OPPONENTS' MAJOR SUIT BID SHOWS 2-SUIT HAND IN THE MINORS. ASKS PARTNER TO BID BETTER MINOR SUIT.

The reasons for competing are covered in the chart on page 65. Keep them in the back of your mind whenever you wish to compete; and remember them as we discuss *how* to compete.

HOW TO COMPETE

The chart on page 66 shows the seven basic ways of competing over an opponent's opening suit bid.

1. THE SIMPLE OVERCALL

When overcalling in a suit, consider these factors:
1. Trick-taking ability is more important than points.
2. Would I be happy if my partner *led that suit to me* in defense?

Consider these two hands.

Your right-hand opponent opens 1 ♡ *and you hold:*

Hand A	(or) Hand B
♠ J x x x x	♠ K Q J 10 x
♡ Q x x	♡ x x x
◊ K x x	◊ A x x
♣ A 10	♣ x x

How many points?	How many points?
What do you bid?	What do you bid?

Which hand would you rather have for an overcall over the opponent's 1 ♡ bid, *Hand A* or *Hand B*?

Including the extra point for a doubleton, each hand contains 11 points.

Hand A, if played in a spade contract, will lose three tricks in spades, at least two and a half in hearts (the queen is not likely to make a trick), two and a half tricks in diamonds, and one trick in clubs. A total of nine losing tricks. At best, therefore, you have a trick-taking ability of four tricks—and it might be as low as three tricks.

In *Hand B*, however, you would lose one trick in spades, three in hearts, two in diamonds, and two in clubs. A total of eight losing tricks, giving you a trick-taking ability of *five* tricks.

Another consideration is that if the opponents win the contract you would be very pleased if partner led a spade in *Hand B*, but not so happy in *Hand A*.

Therefore, although both hands contain 11 points, *Hand B* is a good one spade overcall, and *Hand A* is a poor one. With *Hand A* you would pass; with *Hand B* you would bid one spade.

Examples:

Opponents have opened 1 ◇. What do you bid with these hands?

1. ♠ K Q 10 9 8	2. ♠ 10 8 7	3. ♠ 6 3
♡ 10 6	♡ K 10 9	♡ K Q 3
◇ 6 3	◇ 8	◇ A J 8 2
♣ A 10 3 2	♣ A K J 9 8 6	♣ K 9 6 4
Bid: 1 ♠	Bid: 2 ♣	Bid: Pass

Hand 1. has a good spade suit. An overcall may make life more difficult for the opponents.

Hand 2. has a strong six-card suit with some outside values. It is worth an overcall at the two-level.

Hand 3. though high in point count, has too much of its strength in the opponent's suit and contains no good suit of its own. It is not strong enough for a no trump overcall and therefore a pass is recommended.

RESPONSES TO PARTNER'S OVERCALL

Treat partner's overcall approximately as you would an opening bid. Just be a trifle stronger on a single raise, as indicated on the chart on page 69.

Examples:

The bidding has gone:

Opponent	*Partner*	*Opponent*	*You*
1 ◇	1 ♠	Pass	?

1. ♠ K 10 3	2. ♠ K J 9	3. ♠ J 10
♡ A J 10 9 3	♡ A Q 9 8	♡ A Q 8 7
◇ 7	◇ 6	◇ 8 6 2
♣ 10 9 3 2	♣ J 10 9 8 7	♣ J 9 8 6
Bid: 2 ♠	Bid: 3 ♠	Bid: Pass

RESPONSES TO PARTNER'S OVERCALL

WITH A BAD HAND...

WITH SUPPORT FOR PARTNER:

8 TO 10 POINTS  I RAISE ONE LEVEL!

11 TO 13 POINTS I RAISE TWO LEVELS!

14 POINTS I RAISE TO *GAME!  *IN A MAJOR SUIT

H.L.

■ WITH NO SUPPORT IN PARTNER'S SUIT, BUT WITH A <u>VERY GOOD</u> SUIT OF YOUR OWN, BID YOUR OWN SUIT. ■ WITH GOOD CONTROLS IN OPPONENT'S SUIT, YOU MAY BID NO TRUMP... (1NT, 2NT OR 3NT DEPENDING ON STRENGTH) ■ CUE BID IN OPPN'T'S SUIT IS ONLY FORCING BID.

4. ♠ 6
♡ A Q J 10 8 7
♢ 7 5
♣ K 6 4 2

Bid: 2 ♡

5. ♠ K J 10 8
♡ A 9 2
♢ 6 4
♣ A Q 6 4

Bid: 4 ♠

6. ♠ 8 7
♡ 8 7 3 2
♢ A J 10
♣ J 10 9 8

Bid: Pass

WHEN DO YOU RESPOND "NO TRUMP?"

Over partner's overcall do not use a "no trump" bid as a denial. If you do not have support for partner, do not have a very good suit of your own, do not have good controls in opponent's suit, simply say *"Pass!"* Remember, "Pass" is not a dirty word!

A no trump bid over partner's overcall is a positive response. Here's what it says:

I have good controls in opponent's suit and I bid:

One no trump with 8 to 10 high card points,

Two no trump with 11 to 13 high card points,

Three no trump with 14 or more high card points.

2. THE SINGLE JUMP OVERCALL

It is also called "The Intermediate" jump overcall. It requires a very good suit, usually a six-card suit, and 15 to 17 points. With trump support, partner can raise one level with 8 to 9 points, jump to game with 10 or more points.

Example: Over Opponent's 1 ♢ bid, you hold:

1. ♠ A 3
♡ K Q J 10 8 7
♢ 4 2
♣ K Q 3

Bid: 2 ♡

2. ♠ A Q J 10 8 3
♡ K Q 7
♢ A 3
♣ 9 8

Bid: 2 ♠

3. ♠ K 9 8
♡ K Q 4
♢ 9
♣ A K J 10 9 8

Bid: 3 ♣

3. THE ONE NO TRUMP OVERCALL

This is simply the same as an opening one no trump bid, including good controls in opponent's suit. Responder treats it as he would an opening one no trump except that a Stayman bid would be a cue bid in opponent's suit.

Example:

Opponent	Partner	Opponent	You
1 ♢	1 NT	Pass	2 ♢ = (Stayman)

4. THE TAKE-OUT DOUBLE

It is one of the most useful tools in competitive bidding. if used properly it is very effective, but it needs the delicate handling of a Stradivarius. A take-out double is a double made at your first opportunity to call, provided your partner has not made a previous bid (other than pass). It asks partner to bid his best suit.

Examples:

Opponent	You	Opponent	Partner
A. 1 ◊	Double		

Partner	Opponent	You	Opponent
B. Pass	1 ♡	Double	

The above examples are take-out doubles.

Partner	Opponent	You	Opponent
C. 1 ♣	1 ◊	Double	

Example C is *not* a take-out double. Partner has already bid. Under the system we are learning, it is a double for penalties. We sometimes refer to it as a "business double."

The basic definition of a hand suitable for using a take-out double is one which is at least equivalent to an opening bid and has support for at least two of the unbid suits.

SHAPE

The more the *shape* of the hand answers this criterion, the less high-card points you need. The poorer the shape of the hand, the more high card points you need.

The ideal hand for a take-out double should have *shortness* and *weakness* in the opponent's suit and *strength* and *length* in the other suits.

Here are examples of ideal shapes of "take-out double" hands, assuming opponents have bid 1 ◊. You will note that good support for the major suits is particularly prevelant.

♠ x x x x x	♠ x x x x	♠ x x x x	♠ x x x x
♡ x x x x	♡ x x x x	♡ x x x x x	♡ x x x x
◊ —	◊ x	◊ x	◊ x x
♣ x x x x	♣ x x x x	♣ x x x	♣ x x x

71

There is one type of hand where you can use the take-out double and not have support for all outstanding suits.

It is a hand that has a strong independent suit of its own and is *too strong* for a simple or a jump overcall, and is *not quite strong enough* for a game-forcing cue-bid. It has a point-count range between 18 to 22 points.

IDEAL TYPES OF HANDS FOR A TAKE-OUT DOUBLE

Opponents have bid: 1 ♦. You can *double* with:

A.	♠ K J x x	**B.**	♠ K Q x x
	♡ A x x x		♡ K J x x
	♦ x		♦ x x
	♣ K J x x		♣ A x x
C.	♠ A Q J x x	**D.**	♠ A K Q 10 9 x
	♡ K Q x x		♡ A Q x
	♦ x		♦ x x
	♣ A x x		♣ K x

The purpose of the take-out double is to request partner to bid his best suit. This he must do even if he has *zero* points!

RESPONSES TO PARTNER'S TAKE-OUT DOUBLE

The accompanying chart indicates the various options the responder has at his disposal. The attitude of the responder is the key to a successful use of the take-out double.

As you must respond with no points, you have to indicate a reasonable hand by jumping in your suit, and stronger hands by the bids indicated on the chart.

Examples: Opponents have opened the bidding with 1 ♦. Partner has *doubled*. What do you bid with:

1. ♠ 9 8 6 3	**2.** ♠ Q 3 2	**3.** ♠ K Q 10 9
♡ 7 6 3	♡ A J 7 6 5	♡ A 6
♦ 9 8 7 6	♦ 6 4 3	♦ J 8 2
♣ 8 2	♣ 9 2	♣ 10 6 3 2
Bid: 1 ♠	Bid: 1 ♡	Bid: 2 ♠
4. ♠ 10 9 6	**5.** ♠ A Q 10 6 3	**6.** ♠ K J 10 3
♡ K 10 8	♡ K J 10	♡ Q J 10 6
♦ A J 10	♦ 8 7	♦ 9 6
♣ 9 6 4 3	♣ K 10 9	♣ K Q 2
Bid: 1 NT	Bid: 4 ♠	Bid: 2 ♦

RESPONSES TO PARTNER'S TAKE-OUT DOUBLE

0 to 8 POINTS: BID YOUR BEST SUIT AT LOWEST POSSIBLE LEVEL.

9 to 11 POINTS: JUMP IN YOUR BEST SUIT.

12 OR MORE POINTS: BID A MAJOR SUIT GAME, OR WITH EQUAL SUITS, CUE-BID OPPN'T'S SUIT.

16 OR MORE POINTS: BID GOOD MINOR SUIT GAME

YOU MAY BID NO TRUMP _ONLY_ IF YOU HAVE _GOOD STOPPERS_ IN OPPONENT'S SUIT AND NO SUIT OF YOUR OWN.

---

8 to 10 POINTS: BID **1 NO TRUMP**

11 to 12 POINTS: BID **2 NO TRUMP**

13 OR MORE POINTS: BID **3 NO TRUMP**

YOU MAY PASS THE DOUBLE _ONLY_ IF YOU HAVE _TREMENDOUS LENGTH & STRENGTH_ IN OPPONENT'S SUIT!

In *Hand 1.* you have a poor hand, but you have no choice. You must bid your "best suit".

Hand 2., although a much better hand, contains only seven high card points. You simply bid your best suit, hearts, at the lowest possible level.

Hand 3., however, has 10 high card points. You indicate that fact by jumping in your best suit, spades.

In *Hand 4.,* with no good suit of your own, but with good stoppers in the opponent's suit and eight points, you bid 1 NT.

Hand 5. is strong enough to jump directly to game in spades.

Hand 6. is very strong, but you are ambivalent as to which suit to choose, hearts or spades. Toss the decision back to partner. Cue bid: 2 ◊, asking him to name *his* best suit.

There are *only two circumstances* where responder may pass:

1. When there is an intervening bid by one of the opponents, you are no longer forced to bid. If you have nothing special to bid, you simply pass.

2. When you have tremendous *length* and *strength* in opponent's suit.

Example:

Opponent	Partner	Opponent	You
1 ◊	double	pass	?

You hold ♠ 3 2
♡ 3 2
◊ K Q 10 9 8 6
♣ A 3 2

With this hand you may pass, converting the take-out double into a penalty double.

DEFENSE AGAINST THE TAKE-OUT DOUBLE

Let's digress for a moment, and put the shoe on the other foot. You are the partner of the opening bidder and the opponent makes a take-out double. Notice the accompanying chart. With 10 high card points or more you *re-double.* You know that from the standpoint of high card points, this is your hand. Partner most likely has at least 12 high card points. You have 10 points. A total of at least 22 points. Your side is stronger than the opponents. You are telling your partner that you can either out-bid the opponents or double them for a profitable set.

WHAT DO YOU DO IF THE OPPONENTS MAKE A _TAKE-OUT DOUBLE_ OVER YOUR PARTNER'S OPENING BID?

PARTNER BIDS:	OPP'N'T. BIDS:	YOU BID:

1. WITH 10 HIGH CARD POINTS OR MORE, YOU ...... **RE-DOUBLE!**

2. ANY OTHER BID IS _NON-FORCING!_ ...INCLUDING ANY JUMP BIDS!

Examples: Partner has opened the bidding with 1 ◊. The opponent then "doubles". What do you bid with:

1. ♠ A Q 8 3	2. ♠ J 4	3. ♠ K J 10 8
♡ K 6 5 2	♡ K J 6 3	♡ A Q 10 6
◊ J 10	◊ A Q 10 4	◊ 6
♣ 9 6 3	♣ 10 9 7	♣ Q J 10 3
Bid: Re-double	Bid: Re-double	Bid: Re-double

With under 10 points and support in your partner's suit you may raise him. Even if you *jump-raise* him, he knows you have less than 10 points. He realizes that if you had 10 points or more you would have re-doubled.

Any other bids are also non-forcing, including jump bids.

Examples: The bidding has gone:

Partner	Opponent	You
1 ♠	Double	?

1. ♠ Q J 7 6	2. ♠ K Q 9 8 7	3. ♠ 8 2
♡ 8	♡ 6	♡ 6 4
◊ Q J 6 2	◊ Q J 3	◊ K Q J 9 8 7
♣ J 10 8 4	♣ 10 9 8 7	♣ 8 4 3
Bid: 2 ♠	Bid: 3 ♠	Bid: 3 ◊

5. CUE-BID

The opponent's have opened the bidding, but you have a very powerful hand—so strong that you would like to be in a game contract. You signify that circumstance by cue-bidding the opponent's suit. Example of this type of cue-bid:

You hold: ♠ K Q J 9 6
         ♡
         ◊ A K J 7
         ♣ K Q J 2

Opponent	You
1 ♡	2 ♡

This cue-bid acts as a super take-out double. Partner may not pass. He responds to your cue-bid by bidding his best suit.

6. PREEMPTIVE OVERCALLS

This type of bid is used to upset the flow of information between the opponents. It "preempts" the opponents.

The hand should contain at least seven cards in one suit, and have less than opening bid high-card strength. Your trick-taking ability should be within three tricks of your bid if you are non-vulnerable, and within two tricks if you are vulnerable. The best type of preemptive bid is one in which your high card strength is in your long suit rather than outside it.

Examples of preemptive jump overcalls:

Opponents have opened the bidding with 1 ♣.

You Hold: **A.** ♠ K Q J 10 8 7 6   **B.** ♠ 5
            ♡ J   ♡ K Q 10 9 8 7 4
            ◇ 10 6 3   ◇ A 10 7 6
            ♣ 6 2   ♣ 3
        Bid: 3 ♠   Bid: 3 ♡

7. THE "UNUSUAL" NO TRUMP

This is a conventional bid that can be used effectively with the right kind of hand, when the opponents make an opening bid in a major suit, and partner has not previously bid. A two no trump jump overcall describes a hand containing two minor suits of at least five cards each.

Examples:

You hold: ♠ x x
             ♡ x
             ◇ A J x x x
             ♣ K Q x x x

The bidding has gone:

Opponent	You bid:
1 ♡	2 NT

or

Partner	Opponent	You bid:
Pass	1 ♡	2 NT

Partner is asked to bid his *better minor suit.*

Example responses to partner's unusual no trump:

Opponent	Partner	Opponent	You
1 ♡	2 NT	Pass	?

Hand A
♠ Q J 4 2
♡ Q 5 2
◇ K 4
♣ 9 8 6 3
Bid: 3 ♣

Hand B
♠ Q J 8 7 5
♡ K x x
◇ 8 7 6
♣ 8 3
Bid: 3 ◇

The unusual no trump can also be used over a minor suit opening by the opponents. It shows a two-suited hand containing the *lower ranking* of the outstanding suits.

Examples:

Opponent	You	
1 ◇	2 NT = two-suited hand containing clubs and hearts.	
1 ♣	2 NT = two-suited hand containing diamonds and hearts.	

BIG HAND BIDDING

Occasionally a hand comes up where you can practically guarantee game in your own hand. When the hand is suitable for a suit contract, your opening bid is *two* of the suit. The accompanying chart indicates the opening bids and responses. The beauty of the opening two-bid of a suit is that it is forcing to game, and you can investigate the possibilities of slam slowly without fear of being passed out.

Examples:

Typical opening two-bids in a suit:

1. ♠ A K Q 10 9 8
♡ A K 8
◇ K Q 7
♣ 8
Bid: 2 ♠

2. ♠ K Q
♡ K Q J 10 8
◇ A K Q 6
♣ A 3
Bid: 2 ♡

3. ♠ 7 5
♡ A Q J
◇ A K
♣ A K Q J 10 3
Bid: 2 ♣

BIG HAND BIDDING!

OPENING 2-BID IN A SUIT SAYS:

> PARTNER, WE CAN BID AND MAKE GAME, EVEN IF YOU HAVE *NOTHING!* THEREFORE, YOU MAY *NOT PASS* UNTIL GAME IS REACHED OR THE OPPONENTS ARE DOUBLED!

OPENER SHOULD BE WITHIN ONE TRICK OF GAME IN HIS OWN HAND.

2♠ OR 2♥ =
25 POINTS WITH GOOD 5-CARD SUIT
23 POINTS WITH GOOD 6-CARD SUIT
21 POINTS WITH GOOD 7-CARD SUIT

(2♦ OR 2♣ REQUIRES 2 EXTRA POINTS)

RESPONSES: 6 POINTS OR LESS, SAY 2 NT

7 POINTS OR MORE:

■ RAISE PARTNER WITH SUPPORT IN HIS SUIT.
■ BID 5-CARD SUIT HEADED BY 3 POINTS.
■ BID 3 NO TRUMP.

Responses to partner's opening two-bid in a suit.
Partner has opened with a 2 ♠ bid. What do you bid with:

1. ♠ J 3	2. ♠ J 3	3. ♠ J 6 3
♡ Q 7 6	♡ K Q 7	♡ K J 9 2
◇ Q 10 9 8	◇ Q 10 9 8	◇ Q 7 6 3
♣ J 6 4 2	♣ 9 8 7 6	♣ 8 2
Bid: 2 NT	Bid: 3 NT	Bid: 3 ♠

4. ♠ J 2	5. ♠ J 10 2	6. ♠ 7 6
♡ Q J 9 8 3	♡ 9 2	♡ A 7 6 5
◇ K 8 7 2	◇ K J 10 8 7 3	◇ K J 10 9 8
♣ 6 3	♣ Q 2	♣ 6 2
Bid: 3 ♡	Bid: 3 ♠	Bid: 3 ◇

THE BLACKWOOD CONVENTION

One of the methods of determining whether you have sufficient controls (aces and kings) for slam, is the Blackwood convention.

Use the Blackwood convention when the only question you need answered is whether the partnership has sufficient aces to enable you to successfully bid a slam.

Bid four no trump which asks partner to tell you how many aces he has.

The responses are simple.

With no aces, partner makes the lowest bid available, "Five clubs."

With one ace, "Five diamonds." Two aces, "Five hearts." Three aces, "Five spades."

With all four aces, there is a variance. The bid is "Five clubs." (You will notice that it is the same bid as having no aces.) Partner should know from the content of his hand, and from previous bidding whether it means all four aces or no aces.

The reason for this variance is to keep the "five no trump" bid available to the Blackwood initiator to ask for kings.

If the initial response to Blackwood shows that the partnership has *all the aces,* and the Blackwood initiator wishes to explore further for a grand slam, he can then ask for kings by bidding, "Five no trump."

Here the responses are straightforward, up the line: six clubs = no kings; six diamonds = one king; six hearts = two kings, six spades = three kings; six no trump = all four kings.

BLACKWOOD CONVENTION

4NT PARTNER, HOW MANY <u>ACES</u> DO YOU HAVE?

RESPONSES:

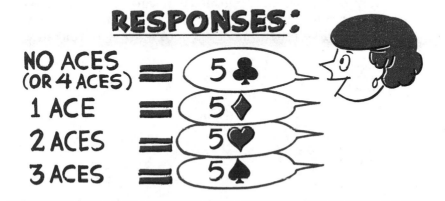

NO ACES (OR 4 ACES)	=	5♣
1 ACE	=	5♦
2 ACES	=	5♥
3 ACES	=	5♠

5NT PARTNER, WE HAVE ALL THE ACES. NOW TELL ME, *HOW MANY KINGS?*

RESPONSES: 6♣ = NO KINGS
6♦ = 1 KING   6♥ = 2 KINGS
6♠ = 3 KINGS   6NT = 4 KINGS

CAUTION: AVOID INITIATING BLACKWOOD:

1. IF YOU HAVE A VOID. **2.** IF A NEGATIVE RESPONSE WILL BRING YOU ABOVE YOUR SUIT AT THE 5-LEVEL. *THIS IS ESPECIALLY TRUE IF YOUR SUIT IS ♣ OR ♦.*

PITFALLS AND PRATFALLS ON THE USE OF BLACKWOOD AND HOW TO AVOID THEM

1. Do not use Blackwood if a negative response will not permit you to play a contract at the five-level.

Example: Your suit is clubs, and you need a response showing two aces for a slam. If partner has only one ace, he would have to bid five diamonds in response to Blackwood. You can no longer play a five-club contract.

2. Avoid using Blackwood when you have a void. When your partner responds to Blackwood, you may have no way of knowing whether one of his aces is in your void suit.

Example:

You	Partner	
	(Hand A)	**(Hand B)**
♠ —	♠ A K Q	♠ K Q x
♡ A K 10 9 8 6	♡ Q J x x	♡ Q J x x
◇ K Q J x	◇ 10 9 x x	◇ A 10 x x
♣ K Q x	♣ J x	♣ J x

Bidding:

(Incorrect use of Blackwood:)

You	Partner	
	(Hand A)	**(Hand B)**
1 ♡	3 ♡	3 ♡
4 NT	5 ◇	5 ◇

(Correct bidding: Cue-bid first-round controls)

You	Partner	
	(Hand A)	**(Hand B)**
1 ♡	3 ♡	3 ♡
3 ♠	4 ♡	4 ◇

(Hand A) Pass
(Hand B) 6 ♡

3. Do not use Blackwood when you have to know *which* ace partner has, not *how many*.

Example:

You	Partner (Hand A)	(Hand B)
♠ A K x x x	♠ Q J 10 x	♠ Q J 10 x
♡ x	♡ A K	♡ Q J 10 x
◇ A K Q J x	◇ x x x	◇ x x x
♣ x x	♣ Q J 10 x	♣ A K

In this example you can make a small slam if partner has specifically the ace of clubs. The ace of hearts does you no good because you could lose two club tricks immediately.

After your partner has responded three spades to your opening one spade bid, you investigate slam possibilities by cue-bidding four diamonds showing first-round control of the suit. If partner responds four hearts, showing the ace of hearts (as in *Hand A*) you sign off by bidding four spades. If partner bids five clubs, showing the ace of clubs (as in *Hand B*), you bid six spades.

As you can see from these examples, a good method of determining controls is by cue-bidding.

4. HOW CAN YOU PLAY A HAND IN FIVE NO TRUMP?

Sometimes, after initiating Blackwood you find yourself in an awkward spot when you learn the opponents have two aces and you have gone past your station. The only solution is to play the hand in five no trump. You cannot bid five no trump yourself because that would be asking for kings. You get around that dilemma by bidding a new suit at the five level *which requires partner to bid five no trump.*

Example:

You	Partner
1 ◇	3 ◇
4 NT	5 ♡
5 ♠	5 NT

5. HOW DO YOU SHOW A VOID WHEN PARTNER HAS BID FOUR NO TRUMP?

We have suggested to avoid *initiating* Blackwood when

you have a *void*. However, suppose partner has initiated Blackwood and *you* have the void. Actually, partner in asking for aces is looking for *first-round* controls; and a void in a suit contract certainly is a first-round control. You indicate a *useful* void by jumping to the six level in the suit which shows how many aces you have.

Example responses:

Partner	You (A)	You (B)
4 NT	5 ◇ = one ace	6 ◇ = one ace + a void
	5 ♡ = two aces	6 ♡ = two aces + a void

A few words of caution. Do not jump to six to show your void if it brings you above your trump suit level. Also make sure your void is *useful*. If you have indications that partner has the ace in your void suit, your void is *not* a useful void.

THE GRAND SLAM FORCE

A very effective convention, but a simple one, is the grand slam force.

It is used in a hand where the determining factor of whether to wind up in a small or grand slam is the content of the trump suit. Does it, or does it not, have all three top honors? When a suit has been agreed upon, and Blackwood four no trump has *not* been used, a bid of five no trump asks partner whether he has *two* of the *top three honors* in the trump suit. If the answer is "yes", he bids seven in the agreed suit; if the answer is "no", he simply bids six in the agreed suit.

BIG NO TRUMP HANDS

There are many hands which are suitable for no trump, but which have more than 18 points. The chart on page 85 shows how many of these hands are bid, particularly the opening two no trump and three no trump bids.

Occasionally there are hands that fall between the one no trump bid (16 to 18 points) and the two no trump bid (22 to 24 points). These 19 to 21 point hands are shown by first bidding a suit and then *jumping* in no trump.

OPENING 2NT BID: (NOT FORCING)

22 TO 24 POINTS WITH BALANCED HAND, ALL SUITS STOPPED. (PARTNER MAY PASS WITH 2 OR LESS POINTS. ANY SUIT BID IS FORCING. A RESPONSE OF 3♣ IS A STAYMAN

OPENING 3NT BID:

25 TO 27 POINTS WITH BALANCED HAND, ALL SUITS STOPPED.

GERBER OVER NT: (ASKS PARTNER FOR ACES,)

I OPENED 1NT OR 2NT

4♣

*GERBER CONVENTION: "HOW MANY ACES DO YOU HAVE?"

RESPONSES ARE:

4♦ I HAVE NO ACES (OR ALL 4 ACES)	4♥ I HAVE 1 ACE
4♠ I HAVE 2 ACES	4NT I HAVE 3 ACES

IF ALL FOUR ACES ARE ACCOUNTED FOR,

5♣ NOW ASKS FOR KINGS

RESPONSES ARE:

5♦ = NO KINGS OR ALL KINGS
5♥ = 1 KING
5♠ = 2 KINGS
5 NT = 3 KINGS

Example:

You	Partner
1 ♣	1 ♡
2 NT	

This bid, although not forcing, gives partner a clear picture of your hand.

THE GERBER CONVENTION

As a response of four no trump to an opening no trump bid is a quantitive bid, it is *not* Blackwood and does *not* ask for aces. Therefore it became necessary to have some other method of asking for aces (and then later for kings).

John Gerber came up with a solution many years ago; and not so strangely it is called the Gerber Convention.

A response of four clubs to an opening one no trump or two no trump bid asks for aces. The dialogue is indicated in the chart on page 85. Similarly, if all the aces are accounted for, five clubs asks about kings.

PREEMPTIVE BIDDING

One of the fun aspects of the game is to make life difficult for the opponents.

If left to their own devices, a reasonably good partnership can often reach their best contract. But with good interference by the opposition, even experts sometimes falter.

A preemptive opening bid of three or more in a suit eats up a lot of bidding room, and cuts down the amount of communication between the opposing partners.

What then are the requirements of such a preemptive bid?

Firstly, the hand should be below an opening bid in high card strength. Secondly, whatever high cards you *do* have should be mainly in your long suit. Basically it means your hand is weak in *defensive* strength, yet strong in playing strength if the contract is played in your suit. Here is typical preemptive bid.

♠ K Q J 10 x x x
♡ x x x
◇ x x
♣ x

Your opening bid would be "three spades".

A preemptive bid is more advisable in third position, because your partner has already passed. In first or second position you may be preempting your own partner, as well as the opponents.

When making a preemptive bid, make it as high as you safely can. The higher you can make the bid, the less room the opponents have to communicate with each other. they may overbid, underbid, or wind up in the wrong suit.

As a general guideline, the trick-taking ability of your hand should be within two tricks of your bid when you are vulnerable, three tricks when you are non-vulnerable.

HOW DO YOU DEFEND YOURSELF AGAINST A PREEMPTIVE BID?

There are many methods of dealing with opponents' preempts. None of them is completely satisfactory. Preemptive bids are designed to make life difficult for the opponents, and they do.

The methods we suggest here are relatively simple, but a great deal of judgment still has to be exercised.

A double of an opening three-bid is optional (partner may bid or pass depending upon the type of hand he has). Ideally, the doubler should have a very good hand and tolerance for all the unbid suits.

An overcall in a suit indicates a good suit and a reasonably good hand. Remember, you are entering the bidding at the three level or higher.

A game-forcing bid is a cue-bid in the opponent's suit.

Example:

Opponents	You
3 ♣	4 ♣

It asks partner to bid his best suit.

A preempt at the four level creates more difficulty.

A double, though optional, is more likely for penalties than for take-out.

A double of four spades is definitely for penalties, because the four no trump bid is available for take-out.

Over a four heart preemptive bid, four no trump basically asks for a minor suit preference. Over a four spade bid, four no trump is for take-out. It does not rule out the possibility of hearts, although it is primarily for the minor suits.

Over opponent's three heart or three spade preempt, a three no trump bid indicates a willingness to play at a no trump contract. Four no trump is the "unusual no trump" asking for partner to bid his better minor suit holding.

Examples:
Here are some examples of defense against opening preempts. Opponents have opened with a 3 ♣ bid. What do you bid with:

1.	♠ K 6 3	2.	♠ A Q J 9	3.	♠ A K Q 10 9
	♡ A K Q 10 9 6		♡ K Q 10 6		♡ A K J 10 3
	◇ J 4		◇ K 10 3		◇ K 3
	♣ 6 3		♣ 7 2		♣ 6
Bid: 3 ♡		Bid: Double		Bid: 4 ♣	

PENALTY DOUBLES

We all are aware of the rewards for bidding and making contracts. But bonanzas can also be gained by defeating the opponents, especially when we double them.

We call this type of double, "a penalty double" or we often refer to it as a "business double."

Some of these penalty doubles are made at fairly high level contracts.

Sometimes we arrive at a major suit game contract and the opponents compete by bidding five of a minor suit. If we feel we may not be able to make 11 tricks in our suit but can defeat the opponents, we "double" their bid.

Example:

North-South are vulnerable; East-West, non-vulnerable.

North
♠ K 10 5 3 2
♡ A 6 4 3
♢ Q J
♣ K 6

West
♠ 6
♡ 8 7
♢ A 9 8 7 6
♣ Q J 10 8 7

East
♠ 9 7
♡ Q J 9 5
♢ K 4 2
♣ 5 4 3 2

South
♠ A Q J 8 4
♡ K 10 2
♢ 10 5 3
♣ A 9

Bidding:

South	West	North	East
1 ♠	Pass	3 ♠	Pass
4 ♠	4 NT	Pass	5 ♣
Double	Pass	Pass	Pass

North and South arrive at a sound 4 ♠ contract. West thinks he might have a "save" at a five-level minor suit contract. He bids 4 NT, asking partner to bid his best minor. East obliges by bidding 5 ♣. South feels that five spades may not make and decides to go for a "sure" profit, by doubling the five-club bid.

As it turns out, South's judgment is correct and West went astray. North-South can make only four spades, but East-West's five club doubled contract is set four tricks for 700 points.

Many sizable profits are made by doubling *low-level* contracts. At low levels many players are prone to "sticking their necks out." They feel "safe" that they won't be doubled at such low contracts.

Significantly, it is precisely at these low contracts that experienced players reap their greatest gains by doubling.

Example: Both sides vulnerable.

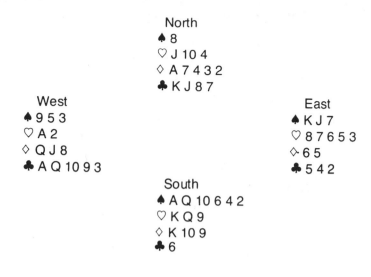

North
♠ 8
♡ J 10 4
♢ A 7 4 3 2
♣ K J 8 7

West
♠ 9 5 3
♡ A 2
♢ Q J 8
♣ A Q 10 9 3

East
♠ K J 7
♡ 8 7 6 5 3
♢ 6 5
♣ 5 4 2

South
♠ A Q 10 6 4 2
♡ K Q 9
♢ K 10 9
♣ 6

Bidding:

South	West	North	East
1 ♠	2 ♣	Double	Pass
Pass	Pass		

Opening lead: ♠ 8

With shortness in his partner's spade suit, North realizes that game is unlikely and seizes the opportunity to double West's 2 ♣ bid. North has at least three defensive tricks and hopes that his partner, with an opening bid, can supply three more. In any event, even if West does make his contract it adds up to only 80 points, which is less than game.

North's opening lead of a small spade sets the stage for a disastrous set. After South wins two spade tricks, he gives his partner a ruff. North cashes the ace of diamonds and continues a diamond to South's king. South leads the king of hearts and eventually North-South win a heart trick and two more trump tricks. The total of eight tricks provides for a three-trick set worth 800 points.

PATTERNS OF PLAY

THERE IS A **RHYTHM**
TO THE PLAY OF THE HAND...

JUST AS IN
**BALLET,
SPORTS,
MUSIC...**

♪ **PLAY WITH A PLAN** ♪

The bidding methods we have been discussing form the basis for arriving at sound contracts. As you continue to play the game you will hear of many bidding systems, new or strange conventions and artificial bids.

Many of these systems are valid methods. The varied conventions and artificial bids may be excellent devices. They work best when they are used properly by experienced players. A simple system used well will succeed more often than an intricate system executed poorly.

At this stage let us try to arrive at good contracts, as simply as possible, and then learn to play the hands as expertly as we can to justify our bidding. In addition, when the opponents obtain the contract, let's defend soundly so we can defeat them, and punish them severely when they over-step their limits.

WHICH BRINGS US TO THE PLAY OF THE HAND

There is a pattern and rhythm to the play of the hand that you can perceive just as in art, music and sports. Watching a master player manipulate his 26 assets is like following a conductor of a giant symphony orchestra who knows every note and nuance of the work plus the capabilities of every instrument and musician.

The key to good playing is good planning. The key to good planning is knowledge of as many factors as we can absorb.

First is any information based upon the bidding, and secondly, any inferences based upon *lack* of bidding.

Then, the knowledge of the various playing techniques available to us is essential to establishing a plan.

We will now discuss some of the most important of these techniques of play.

HOW TRICKS ARE WON

There are basically only three ways of winning tricks.

1. HIGH CARDS

Aces will normally win tricks. Kings can win tricks after the ace has been played, or if the ace is well located.

Combinations of high cards can win tricks. Having both the king and queen in the same suit will usually produce at least one trick. The king may lose to the ace, but the queen now becomes the highest card, thereby winning a trick. The ace and queen combination in the

HOW DO YOU WIN TRICKS

1. HIGH CARDS:

2. LONG SUITS:

3. TRUMPING:

EXAMPLE: HEARTS ARE TRUMP

same suit can also produce one or two tricks depending upon the location of the opposing king.

So we can see that high cards and combinations of high cards can win tricks.

2. LONG SUITS

Long suits can also win tricks. In the example shown, ♣ A K Q 5 4 2, six clubs in one hand, there are only seven clubs available for the other three hands. Assuming an equal distribution among the three hands, they would divide two, two and three. Playing three rounds of the suit, ace, king and queen, would exhaust all the clubs from the opposing hands. This would establish the ♣ 5, 4 and 2 as winners. (This is assuming that the suit is the trump suit; or trumps have all been extracted; or we're in a no trump contract.)

You will note that after the opposing cards in the suit have been extracted, the deuce becomes as strong as the ace was originally.

3. TRUMPING OR RUFFING

In a suit contract tricks can be won by trumping (also called "ruffing") cards in suits in which you are void.

In the example shown in the diagram on page 93, you would win only five trump tricks if you would simply play them out. But by utilizing a "cross-ruff", ruffing alternately spades in one hand and clubs in the other—a total of nine trump tricks will be won.

Although there are only three ways to win tricks— 1. HIGH CARDS, 2. LONG SUITS, 3. TRUMPING—the techniques and maneuvers of accomplishing it are many.

GENERAL TECHNIQUES OF DECLARER PLAY
THE FINESSE

In discussing ways of winning tricks, we mentioned that high cards and combinations of high cards can win tricks. To win a trick with an ace is relatively easy. To win a trick with the king, when the opponents have the ace, is another matter. Trying to win with a queen, when the opponents have the king, or winning with the jack, when the opponents own the queen often require special techniques.

One of these techniques is the finesse.

WHAT IS A FINESSE?

A FINESSE IS AN ATTEMPT TO WIN TRICKS WITH _LOWER CARDS_ BY TAKING ADVANTAGE OF THE FAVORABLE LOCATION OF _HIGHER CARDS_ HELD BY THE OPPONENTS

SOME SIMPLE FINESSES:

	1.	2.	3.	4.	5.	6.
	NORTH	NORTH	NORTH	NORTH	NORTH	NORTH
	A	A	A	A	A	A
	Q	Q	Q	X	X	X
		J	X	X	X	X
	SOUTH	SOUTH	SOUTH	SOUTH	SOUTH	SOUTH
	X	X	J	Q	Q	Q
	X	X	10	J	X	X
		X	X	10	X	

FINESSING AGAINST THE KING

A finesse is an attempt to win a trick or tricks with *lower* cards, based upon the favorable location of a *higher* card or cards held by the opponents.

The finesse is not a sure thing. It is a percentage play. If one of the opponents has the key card, you succeed; if the other opponent has the key card, you fail. But not taking the finesse can often guarantee failure regardless of who holds the key card. A 50-50 chance of success is far better than a 100 percent guarantee of failure.

The first group of diagrams in the chart on page 95 shows six circumstances where a finesse against the king is possible. In the first four examples shown, your *hope* is that the West opponent holds the king. The technique in each of these cases requires that you make the first lead from the South hand.

In the first hand, for example, you hope for this circumstance to enable you to win two tricks in the suit.

```
                        North
                        A Q
        West                            East
        K 5                             9 8
                        South
                        3 2
```

You lead the deuce from the South hand. If West plays the five, you play the queen from the North hand, thereby winning the trick. Subsequently you will, of course, win the ace.

You will note that if West had played the king first, you would have won it with the ace. You would then have been able to win the next trick with the queen.

In the second hand, lead a small card from the South hand. If West plays a small card, play the jack from North. If this succeeds in winning the trick (and it will if West has the king) you would like to repeat the maneuver again. It is then necessary to return to the South hand in another suit.

We have deliberately arranged the example hand on the following page to contain a series of *successful* finesses for the king. It encompasses the first four examples shown in the chart, re-arranged slightly within the North-South hands. North and South by proper finessing techniques can win all 13 tricks in a no trump contract.

```
                          North
                          ♠ A Q
                          ♡ Q J 10
                          ◇ A Q 5 3
                          ♣ 9 6 4 2
        West                                      East
        ♠ K 10 9 8                                ♠ J 7 6 5 4
        ♡ 9 8 3 2                                 ♡ K 7 6
        ◇ K 8 7                                   ◇ 9 6
        ♣ 10 5                                    ♣ K 8 7
                          South
                          ♠ 3 2
                          ♡ A 5 4
                          ◇ J 10 4 2
                          ♣ A Q J 3
```

Assume a three no trump contract by South. West leads the ♠ 10.

Set up the hand and try to play it. Can you win all 13 tricks? Watch your communications between hands so that you can repeat successful finesses. If you don't succeed the first time, look for your errors and try again.

The attempt to win two tricks when the ace and queen are in opposite hands, and do not contain supporting honors, requires a slightly different method.

In this situation:

```
                          North
                          A 3 2
        West                                      East
        J 10 9                                    K 7 6
                          South
                          Q 5 4
```

Play the ace (if you safely can) and then lead the deuce *towards* the queen. If the king comes up, play the five; if a small card is played play the queen, hoping that the opposing king is lying favorably for you.

However, in this situation:

```
                          North
                          A 3 2
        West                                      East
        J 10 9                                    K 7 6
                          South
                          Q 4
```

You cannot afford to play your ace first, because it would "bare" the queen. The queen could then be gobbled up by the opposing king regardless of which opponent held it. Therefore, in this case you lead the deuce. If the king is played, you then play the four. You could then win the queen on the next play of the suit, and subsequently the ace. If East ducks the lead of the deuce, playing the six, you play the queen. In the circumstances shown, you would win the trick with the queen immediately, followed later by the ace.

MORE SIMPLE FINESSES *(See chart page 99)*
Finessing for the ace

1. Lead a small card from South hand.
   If West plays the ace, North plays small.
   If West plays small, North plays the king.
2. In attempting to win two tricks in this combination, South leads a small card. If West plays the ace, North plays small (and the king and queen are established for two tricks).
   If West plays small, North plays the queen. If it holds the trick, South returns to his hand in a different suit and then leads a small card towards North's king.

Finessing for the queen

3/4. If you have sufficient outside entries in the South hand, cash the ace first in the rare hope that the queen might fall singleton. Then return to the south hand via a different suit.

In *Hand No. 3* lead a small card from the South hand. If the queen is not played by West, insert the jack, hoping to win the trick.

In *Hand No. 4* lead the jack from the South hand. If it is not covered by the queen, let it ride. If it is covered, win with the king, thereby making the ten a winning trick.

Hand No. 5 and Hand No. 6 are two-way finesses. You can finesse it either way.

First see if you can get any clues from the bidding or previous play which might indicate who holds the missing queen.

If the indications are that West has the queen, play the ace from the South hand, then continue leading from the South hand in the same manner as in Hands 3 and 4.

MORE SIMPLE FINESSES:

FINESSING FOR THE ACE

NORTH	NORTH
K	K
X	Q
	X
SOUTH	**SOUTH**
X	X
X	X
	X
1.	2.

FINESSING FOR THE QUEEN

NORTH	NORTH	NORTH	NORTH
A	A	K	K
K	K	J	X
J	X	X	X
SOUTH	**SOUTH**	**SOUTH**	**SOUTH**
X	J	A	A
X	10	10	J
X	X	X	10
3.	4.	5.	6.

TWO-WAY FINESSES

DOUBLE-FINESSES
(FOR TWO KEY CARDS)

NORTH	NORTH	NORTH	NORTH
A	A	K	K
Q	J	J	Q
10	10	10	10
SOUTH	**SOUTH**	**SOUTH**	**SOUTH**
X	X	X	X
X	X	X	X
X	X	X	X
7.	8.	9.	10.

RUFFING FINESSES

NORTH	NORTH
A	K
Q	Q
J	J
10	10
SOUTH	**SOUTH**
X	(VOID)
11.	12.

If the clues indicate that *East* has the queen, reverse the procedure. Play the king first from the North hand and finesse towards the South hand.

If there are no clues, your guess is as good as mine.

In *Hand No. 6,* however, you have an extra psychological maneuver. Play the jack from South hand, tempting West to cover with the queen if he has it. If the queen doesn't appear, play the king and then lead up to South's A 10 for the finesse.

THE DOUBLE-FINESSE

The next four examples are typical situations where there are *two* key cards outstanding. In all of them you attempt to win more than one trick in the suit.

Hand Nos. 7 and 8 are finesses which have a 75% chance of succeeding. They lose only when East has *both* outstanding honors. They win when West has both honors, or when the honors are divided between East and West—regardless of which honor it is.

In *Hand No. 7,* it is interesting to note, all *three* tricks can be won if West has both honors. The proper technique is to lead a small card from South. If an honor does not appear from West's hand, play the *ten.* If the ten loses to East's jack, return to the South hand and repeat the finesse again against the king.

Hand No. 9 is simple finesse for the queen. Who has the ace is not a factor. It cannot be prevented from winning a trick. But a trick can be saved if West has the queen.

A small card is led from South. If the queen does not come up from the West hand, insert the ten. If the ten wins, or is captured by the ace, return to the South hand and repeat the maneuver. Lead a small card from South, insert the jack and pray that it wins.

Hand No. 10 contains both a percentage play for the declarer and a psychological ploy available to the defenders.

The proper play is to lead a small card from South. If no honor comes up from West, play the king.

(A) If it loses to the ace, return to the South hand via a different suit. Lead a small card from South and insert the ten, finessing West for the jack. (This maneuver loses only when East has both the ace and the jack.)

(B) If the king holds the trick, return to South hand via another suit. Lead a small card from South, and if no honor comes up from West's hand play the queen. You are finessing West for the ace.

The psychological ploy comes up when the East defender *has* the ace and *smoothly* plays a small card, refraining from winning the trick on the first play of the suit. His play will lead you into the (B) situation causing you to make the "technically correct play" but actually the losing play.

If the defender is good enough to fool you there is not much to do but to congratulate him.

RUFFING FINESSES

This play is available for use in a side suit in a trump contract.

In the examples shown, *Hand Nos. 11 and 12,* you hope that East has the key honor.

In *Hand No. 11,* lead the singleton from South, play the ace from North, then play the queen. If East covers with the king, ruff it and later cash the J, 10. If the king does not appear, discard a loser in another suit.

In *Hand No. 12,* lead the king from North. If East plays the ace you ruff it, setting up your Q J 10. If East plays low, discard a loser in another suit.

ESTABLISHING LONG SUITS

One of the most important ways of winning tricks is by establishing long suits. Sometimes you can win all the tricks. Often you have to lose some to establish the rest.

A common error with beginners is to *block* the suit. This can be prevented by playing the cards in the proper order.

When you have cards of equal value in the same suit you can run the suit by playing the *high cards* first from the hand that has the *fewer cards*. (See chart on next page.)

In *Hand No. 1* the A K Q J and 10 are all *equal*. By playing the king and the ace first you are then able to play the four from the North hand to the queen in the South hand and continue running the suit with the jack, ten and six.

See what happens if you do it incorrectly.

If you were to play the queen first, and then the ace, king, you would run out of cards in the suit in the North hand

101

	1.	2.	3.	4.	5.
	NORTH	NORTH	NORTH	NORTH	NORTH
	A K 4	K Q 3	Q 4	K Q 3	J 3
	SOUTH	SOUTH	SOUTH	SOUTH	SOUTH
	Q J 10 6 3 2	A J 6 5 2	A K J 6 2	J 10 9 6 5 2	K Q 10 5 2

GET ME OUT OF THE WAY, FIRST!

THAT LEAVES PLENTY OF ROOM FOR ME!

H.L.

USUALLY: PLAY THE HIGH CARDS *FIRST* FROM THE HAND THAT HAS THE *FEWER* CARDS!

EXAMPLES:

| GIVE UP **ONE** TRICK TO THE ACE... WIN **5** TRICKS IN THE SUIT! | A. (NORTH) 8 3 (SOUTH) K Q J 10 9 2 | B. (NORTH) A 8 7 5 2 (SOUTH) 6 4 3 | GIVE UP **2** TRICKS, WIN **3** TRICKS IN THE SUIT! | C. (NORTH) Q J 2 (SOUTH) 10 9 8 5 3 |

and have no way of reaching the South hand. You would have *blocked* the suit.

Similarly, in *Hand Nos. 2 and 3* start by playing the high cards from the North hand (the hand with the fewer cards) first. In *Hand Nos. 4 and 5* the same principle applies, although in these cases you first have to concede a trick to the opposition.

GIVE A LITTLE TO GAIN A LOT *(See chart page 103)*

In *Examples A and C* the situation is relatively obvious. In *Hand A* you relinquish a trick to the ace and win the rest of the tricks. In *Hand C* you give up tricks to the ace and king and then win the rest.

In *Hand B*, however, the possibilities are not as easy to see. With eight cards between you and partner, it leaves just five cards with the opposition. Assuming a three-two split, you can still win three tricks, without relinquishing control of the suit, by giving up two tricks as soon as possible. You then win the third round with the ace, exhausting all the opponents' cards in the suit, and establishing the eight and seven as winning tricks.

DECLARER PLAY IN TRUMP CONTRACTS

The time to do your planning is as soon as dummy's hand comes down.

Do your planning *before* you play to the first trick; waiting until the next trick may be too late.

A well-known bridge writer wrote a whole book on errors made on the first trick. The accompanying chart shows some of the factors you have to consider on viewing the dummy.

To add to the arsenal of information on which you can base you plan, determine what you have learned from the opening lead, and what inferences you can make from the opponents' bidding or lack of bidding.

One of the key considerations is:

DO I PULL TRUMPS IMMEDIATELY?

It is often a good idea to exhaust the opponents of their trumps, by playing the trump suit, if you can safely do so and still maintain control of the hand.

The prime reason for pulling trumps is to prevent the

DECLARER PLAY IN
TRUMP CONTRACTS

WHEN DUMMY'S HAND COMES DOWN,
THINK BEFORE PLAYING TO *1ST TRICK*

1. HOW MANY LOSERS DO I HAVE?

2. HOW CAN I GET RID OF THEM?

A. CAN I RUFF THEM IN DUMMY?

B. CAN I THROW THEM OFF ON HIGH CARDS IN ANOTHER SUIT?

C. CAN I SET UP A SIDE-SUIT TO PROVIDE DISCARDS FOR THEM?

D. ARE THERE ANY FINESSES I SHOULD TAKE?

SHOULD I PULL TRUMPS FIRST?

3. WILL MY PLAN GIVE ME ENOUGH TRICKS TO FULFILL MY CONTRACT?

4. DO I HAVE SUFFICIENT ENTRIES TO CARRY OUT MY PLAN?

WHEN TO PULL TRUMPS!

(THAT IS: PLAY THE TRUMP SUIT UNTIL THE OPPONENTS HAVE NO MORE TRUMPS.)

A. YOU DO NOT NEED DUMMY'S TRUMPS FOR RUFFING.

B. YOU HAVE HIGH CARDS OR A STRONG SIDE-SUIT OUTSIDE OF THE TRUMP SUIT THAT YOU DO NOT WANT THE DEFENDERS TO RUFF.

C. YOU HAVE SUFFICIENT TRUMPS TO PULL TRUMPS AND STILL MAINTAIN CONTROL OF THE HAND.

EXAMPLE HAND:

DUMMY

♠	♥	♦	♣
Q	A	J	6
J	K	4	5
4	2	2	3
			2

DECLARER

♠	♥	♦	♣
A	4	A	4
K	3	K	
5		Q	
3		10	
2		3	

CONTRACT: SIX SPADES.
OPENING LEAD: KING♣, THEN ACE♣ IS CONTINUED.

106

opponents from making unnecessary tricks by trumping your high cards in the side suits.

In the example shown on the chart (page 106), declarer can make his contract if he pulls out trump immediately upon obtaining the lead. The contract is assured it the opponents five trumps are divided no worse than four/one.

There are many circumstances, however, when it is wise to *delay* drawing trumps. The accompanying charts indicate some of them.

WHEN TO DELAY PULLING TRUMPS *(See charts pgs. 108-109)*

Hand A. The play might go something like this: Assuming a spade lead, win with the ace and then trump a small spade with dummy's heart three. Cash the club ace; then play a diamond to your ace. Trump another spade with dummy's nine of hearts. Return to your hand by playing a small heart to your ten, and then play your last spade and trump it with dummy's heart queen. Your only losers are a club and a diamond, and you wind up making eleven tricks.

Hand B. If a trump is not led by the opponents, cash the club ace, spade ace and diamond ace. Then alternately play diamonds and spades cross-ruffing the hand, and winding up with eleven tricks.

Hand C. Win the heart ace. Then play the diamond king, queen and ace, discarding the losing heart three from declarer's hand. Only *then* do you play trumps. If all goes well you will lose only the ace of trumps, making your slam contract.

Hand D. Win the heart ace. Cash the queen of trumps. Play the ace, king of diamonds, and ruff a third diamond with trump nine.

If the diamonds break three-three you cash the ace, king of trumps and then play the balance of the diamonds discarding two losers from your hand making eleven tricks.

However, if the diamonds break four-two, you enter dummy by playing a trump to the king. Then trump another diamond with the trump ten. You re-enter dummy by playing a small trump to ace. Then play the last diamond discarding a club or a heart loser from your hand. You wind up making ten tricks.

Hand E. Your only chance of making the contract is if the

WHEN TO DELAY PULLING TRUMPS

A. WHEN DUMMY IS SHORT IN A SIDE SUIT, AND YOU NEED HIS TRUMPS TO RUFF YOUR LOSERS IN THIS SIDE SUIT,

B. WHEN BOTH DECLARER AND DUMMY ARE SHORT IN TWO DIFFERENT SIDE SUITS AND HAND CAN BE PLAYED AS A CROSS-RUFF!

WHEN TO DELAY PULLING TRUMPS (CONTINUED)

C.

C. WHEN YOU NEED TO DISCARD LOSERS IMMEDIATELY ON HIGH CARDS IN ANOTHER SIDE SUIT. (AND YOU'D HAVE TO RELINQUISH THE LEAD IF YOU PLAYED TRUMPS FIRST.)

	TRUMPS			
CONTRACT: 6 SPADES	♠	♥	♦	♣
OPENING LEAD: K♥ DUMMY	J 10 4	8 6 4	A Q 3	J 8 7 6
DECLARER	K Q 9 8 6	A 3	K 2	A K Q 2

D.

D. WHEN YOU NEED DUMMY'S TRUMPS FOR ENTRIES, AFTER SETTING UP DUMMY'S SIDE SUIT.

	TRUMPS			
CONTRACT: 4 SPADES	♠	♥	♦	♣
OPENING LEAD: K♥ DUMMY	A K 3	8 7 6	A K 8 7 6	4 3
DECLARER	Q J 10 9 4 2	A 4 3	4 3	5 2

E.

E. WHEN YOU WISH TO ALTERNATE PULLING TRUMPS AND PLAYING A SIDE SUIT, USING DUMMY'S TRUMPS AS ENTRIES TO TAKE NEEDED FINESSES IN THIS SIDE SUIT.

	TRUMPS			
CONTRACT: 4 SPADES	♠	♥	♦	♣
OPENING LEAD: K♣ DUMMY	A K 3	8 6 5	9 8 7 6	10 8 7
DECLARER	Q J 10 7 6	A Q J	A 3	A 3 2

heart finesse is successful. You must arrange to be able to take the finesse *twice*.

Win the opening lead with the club ace. Cash the spade queen and then the spade king. Play a small heart from dummy and insert the jack from your hand. If the finesse is successful, re-enter dummy with the ace of trumps. Repeat the finesse by playing a small heart from dummy and inserting the heart queen. Now draw any outstanding trumps, cash your outside aces and claim your contract of four spades.

DECLARER PLAY IN NO TRUMP CONTRACTS

The philosophy of declarer play is different in no trump contracts than in trump contracts.

To understand declarer play, we should first look into the hearts of our enemy, the defenders. They are out to beat us. Usually they try to set up their best suit while retaining an outside entry (or entries) to enable them eventually to run their own suit.

Declarer's job is to counteract that plot. He does not have the luxury of a trump suit to stop the opponents' suit. He has to retain stoppers in the opponents' suits (or use other means of preventing the run of their suits) while establishing tricks in his own suits.

When the opening lead is made, the first thing the declarer must do is to determine how many tricks he can win *without* relinquishing the lead. If they do not add up to enough tricks for his contract, he looks around to see how he can establish sufficient tricks, safely.

The following chart shows some of the important factors the declarer must consider when planning his play.

DECLARER PLAY IN
NO TRUMP CONTRACTS

WHEN DUMMY'S HAND COMES DOWN,
THINK BEFORE PLAYING TO 1ST TRICK

1. HOW MANY WINNERS DO I HAVE "*OFF THE TOP*"?

2. HOW CAN I DEVELOP OTHER WINNERS, SAFELY?

3. IT IS MORE IMPORTANT TO DEVELOP **NEW TRICKS FIRST**, BECAUSE THE "TRICKS OFF THE TOP" WILL NOT RUN AWAY!

4. IS THERE A **DANGEROUS** OPPONENT?

5. SHOULD I TAKE THE FIRST TRICK IF I CAN, OR SHOULD I **HOLD UP** ONE OR TWO ROUNDS?

6. DO I HAVE SUFFICIENT ENTRIES TO CARRY OUT MY PLAN?

H.L.

THE HOLD-UP PLAY

The usual strategy for the defenders in no trump play is to try and set up their best suit. They hope to obtain the lead subsequently and then run their suit.

Declarer has to try to prevent this. One of the tools at his command is the hold-up play.

Assuming that the defenders are leading their best suit, the hold-up play is designed to exhaust *one* of the defenders of all his cards in that suit. This will prevent him from continuing the suit if he were to obtain the lead again.

Here is a typical example of the hold-up play:

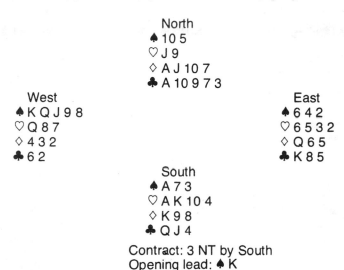

```
                        North
                        ♠ 10 5
                        ♡ J 9
                        ◇ A J 10 7
                        ♣ A 10 9 7 3
        West                                East
        ♠ K Q J 9 8                          ♠ 6 4 2
        ♡ Q 8 7                              ♡ 6 5 3 2
        ◇ 4 3 2                              ◇ Q 6 5
        ♣ 6 2                                ♣ K 8 5
                        South
                        ♠ A 7 3
                        ♡ A K 10 4
                        ◇ K 9 8
                        ♣ Q J 4
```

Contract: 3 NT by South
Opening lead: ♠ K

In this hand, South simply refuses to win the first two tricks. Winning the third spade lead in his hand, South leads the queen of clubs finessing West for the king. Even if the finesse loses to East, (which it does in this particular hand) he now has no spade to return and the contract is assured.

The "DANGEROUS" HAND

HOW TO KEEP THE DANGEROUS DEFENDER OUT OF THE LEAD ...

"DANGEROUS DAN"

"SAFETY SAM"

<u>HAND A</u>

North
♠ K 5
♡ A 7 6
◇ K 10 7 6
♣ Q 5 3 2

West
♠ Q 9 3
♡ J 10 9 8 4
◇ ? 4 2
♣ J 7

East
♠ A J 10 8
♡ 5 3 2
◇ ? 3
♣ 10 9 8 6

South
♠ 7 6 4 2
♡ K Q
◇ A J 9 8
♣ A K 4

Contract: 3 NT by South
Opening lead: ♡ J

SAFETY SAM

<u>HAND B</u>

North
♠ K 10 7
♡ A 6
◇ K 9 8 7
♣ K 9 8 6

West
♠ Q 6 5
♡ K Q 10 9 2
◇ 4 3 2
♣ 7 4

East
♠ 4 3 2
♡ 7 4 3
◇ Q 6 5
♣ Q 5 3 2

South
♠ A J 9 8
♡ J 8 5
◇ A J 10
♣ A J 10

DANGEROUS DAN

Contract: 3 NT by South
Opening lead: ♡ K

THE DANGEROUS OPPONENT

You noticed from the hand just discussed that there was one opponent to whom it was very *safe* to relinquish the lead. Giving the lead to the other opponent was *fatal,* as far as the contract was concerned.

This situation, where there is one *dangerous* opponent, while the other is comparatively safe, comes up quite often in declarer play. This is particularly true in no trump contracts.

Hand A. In this hand you are delighted that you did not get a spade as the opening lead. Your prime concern is to develop tricks so that the spade king cannot be attacked. With an option to finesse the diamond suit either way, play it so that even if you lose, East would be in the lead. He cannot play spades without allowing you to win the first or second trick with the king.

The proper play, therefore, is to play the diamond ace, then lead the jack. If it is not covered, let it ride. Regardless of who has the queen, your contract is safe.

Hand B. After winning the opening lead with the ace of hearts, declarer should play the hand so that East cannot obtain the lead. If West gets into the lead he cannot attack your heart holding without giving you a trick with the jack. However, if East were to lead a heart, *through* your jack-small holding, West could then run the complete heart suit.

So you simply lead from dummy any suit (other than hearts) and finesse against the queen. Even if it loses to West, and he returns a heart, it gives you your ninth trick.

WHICH SUIT DO I SET UP?

In many hands there is a choice of more than one way to play the hand. Which suit do I work on first? What factors should influence my decision? The chart on the next page details some of your considerations.

ENTRIES: MAINTAINING LINES OF COMMUNICATION

Setting up winning tricks in a suit is useless if you can't get into the hand to cash them. Providing for sufficient entries is the answer.

Which Suit Do I Set Up?

OFTEN DECLARER HAS A CHOICE OF MORE THAN ONE SUIT TO ESTABLISH. HERE ARE SOME FACTORS TO CONSIDER TO HELP MAKE YOUR DECISION...

YOU'RE ALL I NEED, BABY!

1. WHICH SUIT CAN PROVIDE _ALL_ THE TRICKS I NEED FOR MY CONTRACT?

2. IN WHICH SUIT CAN I SAFELY BUILD UP THE TRICKS I NEED?

SAFETY ZONE

EVEN IF YOU WIN A TRICK, YOU CAN'T HURT ME!

IF THIS SUIT DOESN'T WORK, I'LL TRY THE OTHER ONE! TWO CHANCES ARE BETTER THAN ONE!

3. IF I TRY ONE SUIT FIRST, AND I AM UNSUCCESSFUL, WILL I THEN BE ABLE TO WORK ON ANOTHER SUIT?

H.L.

Hand 1. Entries in a Side Suit

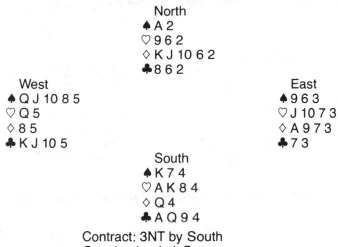

North
♠ A 2
♡ 9 6 2
◇ K J 10 6 2
♣ 8 6 2

West
♠ Q J 10 8 5
♡ Q 5
◇ 8 5
♣ K J 10 5

East
♠ 9 6 3
♡ J 10 7 3
◇ A 9 7 3
♣ 7 3

South
♠ K 7 4
♡ A K 8 4
◇ Q 4
♣ A Q 9 4

Contract: 3NT by South
Opening lead: ♠ Q

It is essential to keep an entry in dummy to run the diamond suit after it has become established. Therefore, the opening spade lead is won in declarer's hand with the king, saving the ace as an entry to dummy.

Hand 2. Entries *within* the suit.

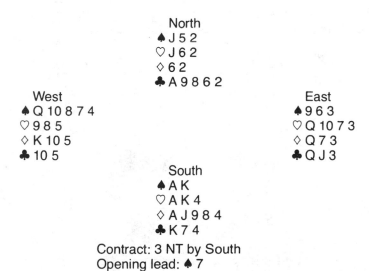

North
♠ J 5 2
♡ J 6 2
◇ 6 2
♣ A 9 8 6 2

West
♠ Q 10 8 7 4
♡ 9 8 5
◇ K 10 5
♣ 10 5

East
♠ 9 6 3
♡ Q 10 7 3
◇ Q 7 3
♣ Q J 3

South
♠ A K
♡ A K 4
◇ A J 9 8 4
♣ K 7 4

Contract: 3 NT by South
Opening lead: ♠ 7

After winning the opening lead, declarer plays the ♣K, and then gives up the next club trick. The ♣A is available in dummy to run the balance of the suit.

OPENING LEADS

A CASE FOR THE DEFENSE

The declarer has a tremendous advantage over the defenders. The opening leader has to make his first play "a shot in the dark". He sees only his own thirteen cards.

The declarer, however, before he is required to play, sees the opponents' opening lead plus *100 percent* of his assets: The combined 26 cards of the partnership, his and his partner's hands.

THE OPENING LEAD

Although a defender starts out "in the dark" he does have the advantage of striking the first blow. If he hits a vital spot, he can often destroy what might otherwise be an ironclad contract.

So the opening lead is the defenders' most important weapon. It is the beginning of the defense. At the same time it starts the communication process between the partners—who cannot see each other's cards.

In determining which card to lead, the defender should evaluate all the evidence available.

1. What information has he learned about the opponents' bidding? . . . location of high cards? . . . distribution? . . . point count of opponents' hands?

2. What has he learned from partner's bidding?

3. What inferences can he make from "lack of bidding?"

Based upon these threads of evidence, and upon the character of his hand, the defender decides which suit to lead.

Having determined the suit, the next thing is to select the correct card. It not only must be the most effective card, but it must also try to communicate his holding in the suit to his partner.

A logical system of play is necessary to simplify this understanding. The method we are recommending is widely used, and is therefore most readily acceptable in social play. No great dissertation has to be made in advance to have partnership understanding.

As you gain more experience in the bridge world you will be exposed to variations in defensive play systems. You will hear such phrases as "Journalist leads," "Rusinow leads," "mud leads," "jack denies, ten implies," "ace from A K x," etc. These are all valid methods when they are *understood* and adhered to by *both* members of the partnership. There is no point in being exotic just for the sake of being exotic.

NO TRUMP LEADS

WHEN LEADING YOUR OWN BEST SUIT: (BLIND LEADS)	WHEN LEADING PARTNER'S BID (OR IMPLIED) SUIT:

WHEN LEADING YOUR OWN BEST SUIT: (BLIND LEADS)

A. TOP OF A SEQUENCE:

K Q J 10

Q J 10 X X

J 10 9 8

B. TOP OF INTERIOR SEQUENCE:

A Q J 10

A J 10 9

A 10 9 8

K J 10 9

C. FOURTH BEST OF YOUR LONGEST and STRONGEST SUIT:

Q J 7 6 5

K J 6 3

WHEN LEADING PARTNER'S BID (OR IMPLIED) SUIT:

WITH 3 OR MORE CARDS:

A. HEADED BY ONE HONOR OR BY TWO NON-TOUCHING HONORS LEAD LOWEST CARD (OR 4th BEST CARD).

A X X X

Q X X

K 10 X X

Q 10 X

B. HEADED BY TOUCHING HONORS, LEAD HIGHEST CARD.

Q J X X

K Q X X

J 10 X

WITH SMALL CARDS:

A. 4 CARDS, LEAD LOWEST.

7 6 4 3

B. 3 CARDS, LEAD HIGHEST

8 6 2

WITH ANY 2 CARDS, LEAD HIGHEST.

K X

4 2

So let's keep our defensive play simple and make life easy for our partners.

Because the defense philosophy is different for no trump and suit contracts, we have divided our chart into separate categories.

In addition, there is a differentiation between "blind leads" and leads of partner's suit.

"Blind leads" are those where partner has not bid and you are leading solely on your own hand.

NO TRUMP LEADS

It is usually wise for the defenders to try to develop their strongest suit as quickly as possible. Whenever the strong suit has a sequence (such as, Q J 10 5 3 or K Q J 6 2) lead the *top* card of the sequence.

When the suit has a broken sequence (such as, K Q 10 9, Q J 9 8 or J 10 8 7) treat it as a complete sequence and lead the top card.

When the suit has an interior sequence (such as, A Q J 10, K J 10 9 or A J 10 9) lead the top of the interior sequence.

When you want to lead your best suit, and it does not contain such sequences, lead the *fourth* card down from the top.

For example: From A J 8 7, lead the seven. From K 9 6 5 4, lead the five. This "fourth best" lead permits the utilization by partner (and by the declarer as well) of the Rule of Eleven.

THE RULE OF ELEVEN WORKS LIKE THIS:

If your partner has led his "fourth best" in a suit, you subtract that card from 11. This will tell you how many cards *higher* than the card led there are outside the leader's hand.

If partner has led the five of diamonds, for example, you subtract 5 from 11 and come up with 6. You know that there are *six* cards higher than the five outside the leader's hand.

If dummy has ◇ Q 9 4 and you hold ◇ K 10 7, you can *see* five cards higher than the ◇5. Therefore you *know* that declarer can have only *one* card higher than the five. You now can judge your proper play based on this information. If you assume declarer has an honor, you can safely play the seven, when dummy plays the four, forcing out declarer's honor.

121

OPENING LEADS
AGAINST SUIT CONTRACTS

WHEN LEADING PARTNER'S BID (OR IMPLIED) SUIT:	BLIND LEADS: (PARTNER HAS NOT BID)

WHEN LEADING PARTNER'S BID (OR IMPLIED) SUIT:

|A| X X X

|K| Q X X

Q X X |X|

Q |J| 10

Q 10 |X|

K X |X|

|K| X

|J| X

|7| 5 2

|4| 2

|3|

BLIND LEADS: (PARTNER HAS NOT BID)

HIGHEST CARD IN A SEQUENCE

|K| Q J

|Q| J 10

|J| 10 9

|K| Q 10

|Q| J 9

|J| 10 8

FROM AK COMBINATIONS:

A |K| X (SUIT CONTAINING 3 OR MORE CARDS)

A |K|. PLAYING ACE, THEN KING SHOWS A DOUBLETON.

AVOID LEADING FROM THESE TYPES OF COMBINATIONS:

A Q J

A J 10

K J 10

When partner has bid a suit (or implied a suit through a take-out or business double) and you wish to lead that suit, the suggested procedure is indicated on the chart.

Leading partner's suit is usually a very good idea, both tactically and for maintaining partnership confidence and morale.

OPENING LEADS IN SUIT CONTRACTS

The strategy in defending against suit contracts is different than in no trump. Developing a long suit by the defenders is usually useless (unless the defense can obtain control of the trump suit). By the time you have established it, declarer's side can prevent the running of the suit by trumping it.

The strategy generally is:
1. Establish high card winners
2. Obtain ruffs
3. Shorten declarer's trumps to fewer than defenders.
4. Prevent ruffing of your high cards.

ESTABLISHING HIGH CARD WINNERS

When you are defending, and your partner has bid a suit, it is usually a good idea to lead that suit. You want to be able to establish and cash those high cards quickly before declarer has a chance to discard his losers in that suit.

If you have good high card sequences, such as K Q J, K Q 10 9 or Q J 10 it is usually a good idea to lead the top card to establish the lower cards as quickly as possible.

It is generally more important to *establish* high card winners, than to merely cash high cards that you happen to have at hand.

For example, you are on lead with this hand. The opponents are in a four spade contract and your partner has not bid.

♠ x x
♡ K Q J x
◇ A x x x
♣ A x x

Suppose you were to lead your two aces first, and then play your ♡ K. True, you would win two tricks right away, but then declarer might easily discard his losing hearts on established clubs and diamonds that you so graciously set up for him.

Look what happens when you lead ♡ K first, with the opponents having this setup.

Dummy
♠ A K x
♡ x x x
♢ Q x
♣ J 10 x x x

Declarer
♠ Q J 10 x x
♡ A x x
♢ K J 10
♣ K Q

Declarer cannot set up either his clubs or diamonds without relinquishing the lead to you. You will then cash your high ♡ Q and ♡ J as well as the ♢ A and ♠ A, winning four tricks and setting the contract.

HOW TO OBTAIN RUFFS

Leading partner's suit when you have a singleton or a doubleton will often permit partner to win his high cards first and then give you a ruff.

Leading a singleton in a suit not bid by partner can be effective if used properly and very dangerous if not.

Do lead a singleton if you have first or second round control of trump and you have a way of reaching partner in another suit.

Do lead a singleton if you have reason to believe partner has the ace, or that it is his suit.

Do not lead a singleton if you do not have first or second round control of the trump suit.

Do not lead a singleton if it will establish opponent's suit.

Do not lead a singleton if you will be ruffing with trumps you would win anyway.

WHEN TO SHORTEN DECLARER'S TRUMPS

Occasionally you have four or five trumps (or you have reason to believe partner has long trumps) plus a strong side suit. It is often wise to continue playing your strong suit at every opportunity until declarer has fewer trumps than you. This may cause declarer to lose control of the hand and make your side the masters.

WHEN TO LEAD TRUMPS
(Or How to Prevent The Ruffing of Your High Cards)

You will hear many misleading "authoritative" sayings at the bridge table. One of the most common misguided bits of advice to the opening leader is, "When in doubt, lead trumps!"

Leading trumps at the wrong time can be very helpful to the declarer. It can permit him to gain the tempo on the hand and allow him to establish his side suits for discards before you can establish your winning tricks.

But when used properly, an opening trump lead, and continued trump leads by the defense, can be *devastating* to the declarer.

Under what circumstances do you lead trumps?
1. When it appears the declaring side will wish to play the hand as a cross-ruff.
2. When it appears that dummy will be short in a side suit and declarer may want to use dummy's few trumps for ruffing purposes.
3. When you have strength (or tenace positions) in all side suits and a lead of these suits may give up an extra trick to declarer. A typical situation is when you have made an opening no trump bid and the opponents have wound up in a suit contract.

How do you recognize these circumstances? By listening carefully to the bidding and gathering your bits of evidence of the opponents' strength and distribution.

Suppose you are West with this holding:

♠ Q J 10 9
♡ A J 9 8
♢ 5 3
♣ A 6 3

And you hear this bidding:

South	West	North	East
1 ♣	Pass	1 ◇	Pass
1 ♡	Pass	1 ♠	Pass
1 NT	Pass	2 ♣	Pass
Pass	Pass		

What have you learned?

1. The opponents do not have many points. They each made minimum bids and stopped at a very low contract.

2. North must have extreme shortness in hearts because he was afraid of a no trump contract. South must be short in diamonds because he didn't return to diamonds after partner's club support.

3. You have strength in hearts and spades. With declarer's presumed shortness in diamonds, as well as yours, your partner should have at least four diamonds. So your side seems to have control of all the side suits. The only way declarer can make additional tricks is by ruffing. A trump lead is clearly indicated. In order to maintain control, you lead a small club.

When dummy comes down, your analysis is vindicated. Here is the entire hand.

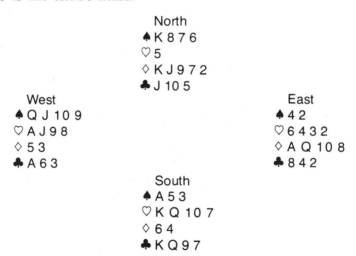

North
♠ K 8 7 6
♡ 5
◇ K J 9 7 2
♣ J 10 5

West
♠ Q J 10 9
♡ A J 9 8
◇ 5 3
♣ A 6 3

East
♠ 4 2
♡ 6 4 3 2
◇ A Q 10 8
♣ 8 4 2

South
♠ A 5 3
♡ K Q 10 7
◇ 6 4
♣ K Q 9 7

Upon winning the club lead in dummy with the ten, declarer leads a heart to his king. You win with the heart ace and plunk down your ace of clubs and follow it with another club. Dummy's trumps are thereby exhausted and the contract is defeated two tricks.

If the defense never led trumps, the contract would be made because dummy could ruff two heart losers.

THIRD HAND PLAY

Until now we have been concentrating on the opening leader in defensive play, but his partner in third position also has an important role to perform. He has to play the

THIRD-HAND PLAY

most *effective* card and at the same time convey as much information as he legally can to his partner.

TOUCHING HONORS OR A SEQUENCE

Your partner has led a low card and you have the ten, jack, queen in that suit. From the effectiveness point of view each card is equal. As far as giving information to your partner, however, it makes a great deal of difference which card is played.

Consider this set-up:

Dummy
◇ 6 5 4

From ◇ K 9 7 2   You hold:
partner has led: ◇ 2   ◇ Q J 10

If you play the ten and declarer wins with the ace, your partner *knows* you hold the jack and queen. (Declarer would have won the trick with the jack or queen if he had them).

If you had played the queen instead, your partner would assume that declarer held the jack and possibly the ten.

So we come to this conclusion:

Whereas we *lead* the *top* of a sequence, *in third hand* we play the *bottom* of a sequence or touching cards.

When partner leads a small card it is generally from a suit containing an honor. Try to determine if it's a "fourth-best" lead. If it is, use the Rule of Eleven and play accordingly.

In third hand it is usually wise to play your highest effective card. It may win the trick or force a high card from the declarer, thereby establishing some of partner's high cards in the suit. (Of course, if there are touching cards adjacent to your highest card, play the lowest of the sequence.)

UNBLOCKING

Getting your high cards out of the way so that partner can run his suit, is called "unblocking!"

We know that when partner is leading a high card from his best suit, it generally contains a sequence. If you have a doubleton containing an honor it is often wise to play it immediately.

128

Example:

You hold A x; partner has led the queen. If dummy's hand does not contain the king, hop up with your ace. (There are times in no trump contracts even when dummy has the king, it is still proper to play the ace). Partner may hold something like Q J 10 x x or Q J 9 8 x. Similarly, if a king is led overtake with the ace and return the suit to partner.

SIGNALLING

As you cannot see each other's cards, you should do whatever you can to help partner make the right decisions in play. Signalling is a legal means of communication between the defending partners. Signals can be used to convey different meanings: attitude, count, suit-preference and lead-direction.

1. ATTITUDE

Your partner has led a suit. You may want him to continue to play that suit or you may not.

If you want him to continue, you first play the *highest* card you *safely* can. If he then plays a card in that suit that retains the lead, you then play your lowest. This "high-low" is a come on. It requests partner to continue playing the suit. If you wish him to discontinue playing the suit, play your lowest card *first*, then the next higher card.

A note of caution: When defending a trump contract, and partner leads the king of a side suit, do not high-low with a queen-doubleton (Q x) unless your hand also contains the jack of the suit. Playing the queen first implies that it is either a singleton, or that the hand contains the jack. Partner can then safely underlead the ace of the suit, knowing that you can either win the trick with the jack or ruff it if the queen was a singleton.

You can also express attitude when discarding. If opponents are playing a suit in which you are void, you can discard high-low in a suit in which you are interested, or low-high in a suit in which you have no interest.

Sometimes you cannot afford a high card in a suit when discarding. Inferentially, you can imply strength in *that* suit by discarding low cards in the *other* suits.

SIGNALS

1. ATTITUDE

I LIKE!

PLAY **HIGH LOW**

PLAY **LOW HIGH**

I DON'T LIKE!

---

2. COUNT

HOLDING AN EVEN NUMBER OF CARDS IN A SUIT, PLAY:

HIGH- LOW

HOLDING AN ODD NUMBER OF CARDS IN A SUIT, PLAY:

LOW- HIGH

---

3. SUIT PREFERENCE

HOW DO I LET HIM KNOW I PREFER DIAMONDS?

TO INDICATE A PREFERENCE BETWEEN TWO SUITS, SIGNAL IN A THIRD SUIT. PLAY A HIGH CARD FOR THE HIGHER RANKING SUIT, YOUR LOWEST CARD FOR THE LOWER RANKING SUIT.

2. COUNT

Many times it is important that partner know how many cards you hold in a suit. You play *high-low* in suits you hold an even number of cards, and "up-the-line" (low-high) in suits you hold an odd number of cards.

For example, if your partner or the opponents lead a suit in which you hold 8 4 3, and you want to show your count, you first play the three and then the four. If you had held 8 4, you would have played the eight first and then the four high-low, showing an even number of cards.

3. SUIT-PREFERENCE

The suit-preference signal is a very handy gadget if used wisely. It is particularly useful in suit contracts. There are times when you wish to tell partner which of two suits to lead. You indicate your choice by your play in a *third suit*.

You play the highest card you can spare to indicate the higher ranking of the two suits; the lowest card for the lower ranking suit.

Example: Bidding has gone:

West	North	East	South
1 ♡	1 NT	2 ♡	4 ♠

You lead the ace of hearts and dummy comes down:

North (dummy)
♠ A J 6
♡ K Q 7
♢ K 8 7
♣ K 8 7 6

West (you)
♠ K 2
♡ A 10 6 4 2
♢ Q 10 9
♣ Q J 10

You are unhappy to see the king, queen of hearts in dummy, but you are delighted that declarer follows suit with the five of hearts. You know from the bidding that to continue hearts is futile; declarer would discard his losers on the high hearts. You have to switch to diamonds or clubs immediately. But to which suit?

Without help from partner you are on a pure guess. But partner was kind enough to have played the *jack* of hearts on the first trick—the suit preference signal. Between diamonds and clubs he wants you to play the *higher* ranking suit, diamonds. So you lead the diamond queen, and the suit is continued until you've won three tricks in the suit, defeating the contract.

Here is the entire hand:

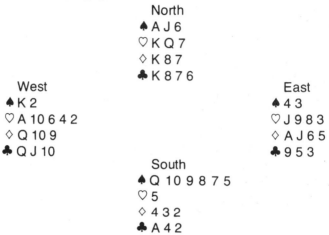

```
                        North
                        ♠ A J 6
                        ♡ K Q 7
                        ◇ K 8 7
                        ♣ K 8 7 6
        West                            East
        ♠ K 2                           ♠ 4 3
        ♡ A 10 6 4 2                    ♡ J 9 8 3
        ◇ Q 10 9                        ◇ A J 6 5
        ♣ Q J 10                        ♣ 9 5 3
                        South
                        ♠ Q 10 9 8 7 5
                        ♡ 5
                        ◇ 4 3 2
                        ♣ A 4 2
```

If East had held the ace of clubs instead of the ace of diamonds he would have played the three of hearts on the first trick. This would have indicated a desire for the lead of a club, the *lower* ranking suit. Under those circumstances West would have led the queen of clubs, instead. This also would have resulted in a one trick set.

Another use of the suit-preference signal is when you are giving partner a ruff in a suit and you want him to return to your hand again so you can perhaps give him another ruff.

Example: Spades are trump and you hold:

```
♠ 10 9
♡ ? 5 3
◇ A K 10 3
♣ ? 5 3 2
```

You play the king and ace of diamonds and partner has shown out on the second round. You know he can ruff the next trick, but you would like that he put you back on lead so that you can do it again. If you hold the ace of hearts you play the ten of diamonds (your higher card) for him to ruff. If you hold the ace of clubs you lead the three of diamonds (your lowest card). Partner should read the leads as suit-preference signals.

LEAD-DIRECTING DOUBLES

Another means of defensive signalling is the lead-directing double.

Double of a No Trump Contract

A double by the partner of the opening leader directs him to:
1. Lead a suit bid by the defending side.
2. If no suit has been bid by defenders, lead the first suit bid by dummy.

Double of a Freely-Bid Slam Contract

It is usually unwise to double a slam contract freely bid by competent opponents. The double of such a slam by the partner of the opening leader has been reserved for lead-directing purposes. It requests partner to make an unusual lead.
1. Lead the first suit bid by dummy (other than the trump suit).
2. If no suit has been bid by dummy, make some other unusual lead.
3. In no case lead a suit bid by the defending partnership.

Double of a Conventional Bid or a Cue Bid

This directs opening leader to lead that suit if the opponents obtain the contract.

For example if the opponents bid two clubs (Stayman convention) and your partner doubles that bid, it requests you to lead clubs if they obtain the contract.

THE STRIP AND END PLAY

HERE'S HOW IT GOES!

STRIP THE OPPONENTS OF KEY SUITS, SO THAT THEY DO NOT HAVE A SAFE EXIT FROM THEIR HANDS. THEN PUT THEM INTO THE LEAD. THEY **END** UP HAVING TO MAKE AN ADVANTAGEOUS LEAD TO YOU.

ADVANCED PLAY

There are some techniques of play that are regular tools in the hands of the expert. But I believe that all serious players should be aware of them. With understanding and application, even beginners should be able to recognize the situations when they occur and execute the play.

THE STRIP AND END PLAY

Once a player has mastered the technique of taking finesses, he then should look around for ways of avoiding them.

Finesses, at best, are percentage plays. Most are 50 per cent plays, some are 25 per cent and some are even 75 per cent. But the good player seeks the "sure thing"—the 100 per cent play. One of the most common methods of avoiding finesses is the strip and end play.

The technique is to *strip* the opponents or your side of certain suits, place the opponents in the lead, and *end* up forcing them to make a lead that changes one of your losers into a winner.

In the example hand you are in a six heart contract. West leads the king of spades.

```
                    North
                    ♠ A 3
                    ♡ Q J 7 6
                    ◊ A J 3
                    ♣ Q 6 5 4
    West                            East
    ♠ K Q 10 9 7                    ♠ J 8 6 4
    ♡ 4 3                           ♡ 8 2
    ◊ ? 7 6 2                       ◊ ? 8 5
    ♣ 9 2                           ♣ J 10 8 7
                    South
                    ♠ 5 2
                    ♡ A K 10 9 5
                    ◊ K 10 4
                    ♣ A K 3
```

You examine your assets and see that you have 11 tricks available "off the top." You win the first trick with the spade ace. After drawing trumps in two rounds, you try to gain your extra trick in the club suit, playing the ace, king and queen. When the suit doesn't break, you ruff the last club in your hand. At this point you are at the crossroads.

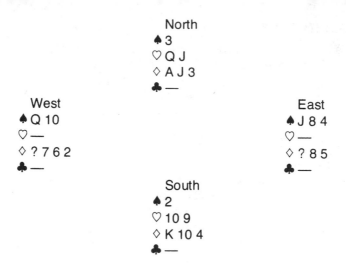

North
♠ 3
♡ Q J
♢ A J 3
♣ —

West
♠ Q 10
♡ —
♢ ? 7 6 2
♣ —

East
♠ J 8 4
♡ —
♢ ? 8 5
♣ —

South
♠ 2
♡ 10 9
♢ K 10 4
♣ —

You can try to guess who has the diamond queen (a 50-50 guess), or you can execute a *strip and end play* (a 100 per cent play).

You have stripped both sides of clubs and the opponents of trumps. You now complete the *stripping* process by playing your last spade. This places the opponents in the lead in the *end* position.

Regardless of who obtains the lead, East or West, the defender must make a losing play. If a spade is played, you ruff in one hand and discard a diamond loser in the other. If a diamond is played, you permit it to come up to the fourth hand, guaranteeing three diamond tricks.

THE SIMPLE SQUEEZE

Occasionally you will find that you are a trick short for the successful fulfillment of your contract. A simple finesse is not available or evidence from the bidding indicates that a finesse will be unsuccessful. This is the time to think of the squeeze play.

In any event it's much more fun to tell friends you made your contract by an exotic squeeze rather than by a lucky finesse.

The basic principle of a squeeze is to create a situation where a defender (or both defenders) has to protect two or more suits, but has to relinquish the protection in one of these suits as you play cards in another suit.

Here is an example of a simple squeeze:

```
                      North
                      ♠ A 3 2
                      ♡ Q J 10 4
                      ♢ Q J 10
                      ♣ A K J
   West                                    East
   ♠ 5                                     ♠ K Q J 9 8 7 6
   ♡ 6 3 2                                 ♡ —
   ♢ 9 7 6 5 3 2                           ♢ 4
   ♣ 5 4 3                                 ♣ Q 10 8 7 6
                      South
                      ♠ 10 4
                      ♡ A K 9 8 7 5
                      ♢ A K 8
                      ♣ 9 2
```

Contract: Seven hearts by South.
Opening lead: Five of spades.

Bidding:

East	South	West	North
3 ♠	4 ♡	Pass	4 ♠
Pass	5 ♢	Pass	5 NT
Pass	7 ♡	Pass	Pass
Pass			

You wind up in a seven heart contract despite interference bidding by East

You count your winners and they add up to only 12 tricks. You have two choices for your 13th trick—a finesse in clubs or a squeeze against East.

You postpone your decision to find out something about the distribution.

After winning the spade ace, you draw trumps in three rounds, noting East's discard of a spade on the first trump. You cash three rounds of diamonds. East shows out on the second round.

Counting out East's hand, you assume seven spades for his bid plus one diamond, leaving room for five clubs. With as many as five cards in the club suit East is more likely to have the queen than West. So you give up the idea of the finesse and go for the squeeze.

You continue playing trumps, the opponents safely discarding until you reach this position:

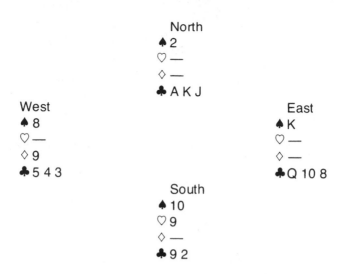

```
                    North
                    ♠ 2
                    ♡ —
                    ◇ —
                    ♣ A K J
   West                              East
   ♠ 8                               ♠ K
   ♡ —                               ♡ —
   ◇ 9                               ◇ —
   ♣ 5 4 3                           ♣ Q 10 8
                    South
                    ♠ 10
                    ♡ 9
                    ◇ —
                    ♣ 9 2
```

You play your last trump. West discards a diamond, north discards a spade, but what can East do? He is squeezed!

He cannot discard the spade king, that will make your ten good. He therefore discards the eight of clubs. But you can now lead a club to dummy, winning the last three tricks with the ace, king and jack.

I want to emphasize three elements that are usually required in a simple squeeze.

1. You should be within one trick of your goal.
2. You need a threat card (or menace card) in at least two suits.
3. In the end position you have the entries to each hand to be able to use the threat cards.

In the hand discussed you had 12 tricks and needed 13. The threat cards were the ♠ 10 and ♣ J. In the end position, you had the lead in your hand to cash the ♠ 10 if East discarded the ♠ K and you could reach dummy with a high club if he discarded the ♣ 8.

COUNTING THE HAND

Incidentally, while we were discussing the "squeeze" hand, we also engaged in the process of "counting out the hand".

This procedure is used by all expert players. It can often reveal the exact distribution of the opponents' hands, and sometimes even the exact cards.

Try to do it. You'll be astonished at how much you will learn about your opponents' cards. It can make you feel as if you've seen all 52 cards.

DUMMY REVERSALS

We are familiar with situations where we pick up extra tricks by ruffing losers in dummy; or to put it more accurately, by ruffing in the hand with the fewer trumps.

Occasionally we can make more tricks by ruffing in declarer's hand (or the hand with the longer trumps) until it has fewer trumps than the dummy. We then use dummy's hand to draw the balance of opponents' trumps.

Example hand: Contract: Four spades by South. Opening lead: ♠ 9.

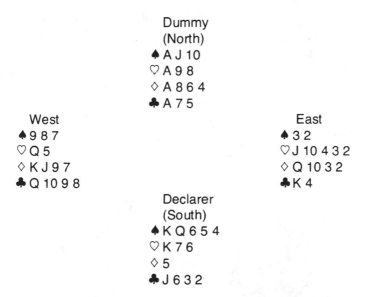

```
                    Dummy
                    (North)
                    ♠ A J 10
                    ♡ A 9 8
                    ◇ A 8 6 4
                    ♣ A 7 5
    West                              East
    ♠ 9 8 7                          ♠ 3 2
    ♡ Q 5                            ♡ J 10 4 3 2
    ◇ K J 9 7                        ◇ Q 10 3 2
    ♣ Q 10 9 8                       ♣ K 4
                    Declarer
                    (South)
                    ♠ K Q 6 5 4
                    ♡ K 7 6
                    ◇ 5
                    ♣ J 6 3 2
```

You have nine tricks off the top. You could attempt to ruff a club in dummy. But that will fail, because the opponents will continue to play trumps each time they get the lead, and exhaust dummy's trumps before you could ruff a club there.

What to do?

Dummy-reversal to the rescue!

By ruffing diamonds in your hand three times, and then using dummy's three trumps for drawing trumps, you wind up with six trump tricks. Added to the ace-king of hearts and the aces of clubs and diamonds you have your ten tricks.

In executing the dummy reversal you have to handle your entries carefully.

After winning the opening trump lead in dummy, play the diamond ace and ruff a diamond in your hand. Play a small trump to dummy's jack, and ruff another diamond with the trump queen. Enter dummy with the club ace, and ruff the last diamond with your king of trumps. Re-enter dummy with the heart ace. Cash dummy's ace of trumps, pulling the last of the opponents' trumps.

A heart to your king gives you the tenth trick.

VIVE LA DUMMY REVERSAL!

FALSECARDING

The elements of play we have been discussing have been pretty much straight-laced. But there is no law against fooling the opponents, if done properly.

One legal, and often effective method of deceiving the opposition is the falsecard. Falsecarding can be done by defenders as well as the declarer.

Falsecarding is playing a card other than in the normal expected order.

In the following hand North and South arrive at a game contract via simple bidding: 1 ♡ by South, 2 ♡ by North, 4 ♡ by South.

```
                         North
                         ♠ 9 4 3
                         ♡ K J 8 4
                         ◇ K Q 7
                         ♣ 8 6 3
      West                                    East
      ♠ K Q 7                                 ♠ 10 8 6
      ♡ 9 5                                   ♡ 7 3
      ◇ 9 8 4 2                               ◇ A J 10 6
      ♣ A 10 9 4                              ♣ J 7 5 2
                         South
                         ♠ A J 5 2
                         ♡ A Q 10 6 2
                         ◇ 5 3
                         ♣ K Q
```

Contract: Four Hearts by South
Opening lead: ♠ K

After studying the opening lead, declarer sees four losers in the hand—two spades, one diamond and one club. The only way to win his contract is with deceptive play in the spade suit.

On the lead of the ♠ K, dummy plays the ♠ 3, East plays the ♠ 6 and declarer *falsecards* by smoothly playing the ♠ 5. West, noticing that the ♠ 2 has not appeared, thinks his partner is giving him an encouraging high-low signal (6-2) to show the ace. He therefore continues playing spades into South's ace-jack combination. Declarer's spade losses are held now to only one trick, permitting North-South to make their contract.

This successful deceptive play by declarer had three elements.

1. *The falsecard.* Playing the ♠ 5 instead of the deuce.
2. *Smooth play.* Unless the plays are made without hesitation, falsecarding will not work.
3. *Declarer executed a play called the "Bath Coup."* Holding an A J x combination, the refusal to win the first lead of the K, in the hope that the suit will be continued, is the Bath Coup.

GO FORTH AND CONQUER

We have tried to cover the basic concepts of the game, providing a simple, workable system of bidding combined with an insight into the play of the cards.

You are now ready to venture forth into the world of social bridge.

Are there more things to learn about bridge? Of course!

But even if you've absorbed just a reasonable percentage of what we've discussed here, you will be able to participate in most social bridge games.

Just one *"don't"* I'd like to warn you about. *Don't* be afraid to play because you think you will make mistakes. Believe me, you *will* make mistakes! But so will all the other players who will play against you.

Actually, *all* players make mistakes. Even the greatest world champions. The only difference is that the better the player, the fewer the mistakes — and the mistakes they *do* make are of a different nature.

YOUR BRIDGE SYSTEM

As you start to play you will hear of many systems and conventions that were not discussed here. Most of them are very fine systems. Most of the conventions work very well when used properly.

However, it is much better to play a simple system well, than a complex system poorly.

You can always include additional conventions as you gain more experience in the game. But don't be in a hurry to add new conventions. It is axiomatic that for every artificial convention you add, you are giving up a natural bid.

If you are asked, "What system do you play?"—your reply is:

"I play Standard American with five-card major suit opening bids; I open the convenient minor when I have to open the bidding with a three-card suit; 16 to 18 point opening One No Trumps; non-forcing Stayman; Blackwood; Gerber over no trump openings; intermediate jump-overcalls; optional doubles over preempts; unusual no trumps for the minors or the lower of the unbid suits.

"In defense, I make standard leads; lead top of nothing from three small cards."

If you are playing with more experienced partners ask them to play your system. They will usually comply.

It is also possible that in some geographical areas you will find players who may be opening "four-card major suits". If that is the case and you want to go along with their wishes, you can modify your system slightly to accomodate them.

Just two variants can take care of it.

1. Do not *support* partner's opening major suit bid with less than four cards in the suit if you can find another suitable bid. If you must support with three cards, they should be at *least* as good as A x x or K J x.
2. Do not *open* a four-card major suit unless you can find a convenient rebid over partner's possible responses.

PROPRIETIES AND PLEASURES

You will get the most enjoyment out of bridge if you consider it a challenging, mind-stimulating game that should be played in a congenial, pleasant, social atmosphere.

The use of common courtesies to partners and opponents alike, plus the strict adherence to a simple code of ethics and the rules of the game make playing bridge more pleasurable.

1. Be nice to your partner. A relaxed partner is a better partner.
2. Be courteous to your opponents. A friendly atmosphere is essential for enjoyable bridge.
3. The code of ethics in contract bridge is different than in other card games.

   Whereas, in poker it is perfectly proper to *act* like you have a good hand when you have a poor hand, or vice versa, in bridge your cards have to do the talking, not your actions.

   You cannot, for example, hesitate as if you're considering which card to play when you hold only a singleton; or if declarer leads a queen it is improper to hesitate perceptibly as if you were considering the play of the king, when you do not hold that card.
4. Play each card and make each bid with the same emphasis.
5. While you sometimes have to take time to consider your proper bid or play, you may not use this method to either convey information to your partner or to deceive the opponents.

6. Do not remove a card from your hand until it is your turn to play. It is both ethically and tactically wrong.

7. Do not indicate either approval or disapproval of bids or plays during the game.

8. Do not discuss either bidding or play during the course of the hand. Wait until play is completed.

9. When you are dummy, do not look at partner's or opponents' hands. You will automatically lose certain rights.

   Your rights and duties as dummy are considerable. They can prevent partner from making two costly mistakes.

   a. You can prevent partner's lead from the wrong hand by saying, "The lead's in dummy." or, "The lead's in your hand."

   b. You can prevent a revoke* by asking partner, when he fails to follow suit, "No spades, partner? (or whatever the suit happens to be)"

*A revoke is made when a player fails to follow suit to a trick while he *does* have a card in that suit. It becomes an estabished revoke if it is not corrected before the offender's side plays to the next trick. The penalty to the offending side can be as much as the loss of two tricks.

10. Follow the rules—even in a "friendly" game. If you enforce *some* rules and not others you get into a situation of "which rules do you follow and which do you not?" It is better to follow *all* the rules.

   To cover all the rules of the game in this book is impossible. To cover them partially would wind up covering them inadequately.

   A good idea is for one person in your group to own a book on the rules of contract bridge. It is published by the American Contract Bridge League.

HAVE FUN

Be serious about your bidding. Be serious about your play. But above all, as you continue to learn and play the game of bridge, have fun.

**Playing In The Real World of Bridge
(or how the other half lives)**

You now have in your hip pocket an excellent, viable method of bidding and play. It is the system that most social bridge players use. As you continue to play the game, you will run into some conventions, systems and styles of bidding that seem strange to you. Sometimes, you may even say to yourself, "Hey, what does that mean?" Actually, at your turn to bid, you may ask it *out loud* of the partner of the opponent that has made the bid.

To give you an insight into what is around, we will go over some of the more popular conventions and bidding methods now in use. Some of them are different than the methods we have learned. Some of them are merely additions. If you feel comfortable with any of these methods or conventions you may want to adopt them. If not, at least you will be aware of them.

THE WEAK TWO BID

Many players, particularly those playing duplicate bridge, use an opening bid of two diamonds, two hearts or two spades as a preemptive bid. It designates a hand that is *below opening bid strength*, but which contains a good six card suit. The standard point range of such a bid is 6 to 12 high card points. (I recommend a top limit of 11 points, because with 12 points I prefer an opening bid of one in the suit.)

I HAVE A GOOD SIX CARD SPADE SUIT AND LESS THAN OPENING BID HIGH CARD STRENGTH... 2♠

THE WEAK TWO BID CAN BE A POWERFUL TOOL.

Examples:

♠ J 5   ♠ K J 10 9 8 6   ♠ 5 4
♡ K Q 10 9 7 6   ♡ 10 7   ♡ 7 6
◇ 10 7 6 5   ◇ A Q 7   ◇ K Q J 10 9 7
♣ 6   ♣ 9 6   ♣ A J 6
Bid: 2 ♡   Bid: 2 ♠   Bid: 2 ◇

RESPONSES TO PARTNER'S OPENING WEAK TWO BIDS

When responding to partner's opening weak two bid, you should decide whether or not game is possible.

If game is not possible, then there are other considerations: Do you think the *opponents* can or cannot make game.

If you believe they *cannot* make game, a good idea is to pass. If you believe the opponents *can* make game, it is okay to simply pass, or to continue the preempt, if you can safely do so.

	partner	opponent	you
	2 ♡	pass	3 ♡
or	2 ♡	pass	4 ♡

If game is possible, the usual forcing bid response is 2 NT, asking partner to describe his hand.

The simplest method of replying to the 2 NT forcing bid is for the opening two-bidder, with a 9 to 11 point hand, to show a "feature," an ace or a king in a side suit, by bidding that suit. With a lesser hand and/or no feature, he simply rebids his original suit.

Examples:

♠ K Q J 7 6 5   ♠ 9 8   ♠ 6 5
♡ 7 5   ♡ K J 10 9 7 6   ♡ J 5
◇ A 8 7   ◇ Q J 9 8   ◇ K Q J 9 8 7
♣ 9 8   ♣ 10   ♣ K 10 6

Opening bidder	Responder	Opening bidder	Responder	Opening bidder	Responder
2 ♠	2 NT	2 ♡	2 NT	2 ◇	2NT
Rebid: 3 ◇		Rebid: 3 ♡		Rebid: 3 ♣	

There are times when you feel that game is likely regardless of whether partner has opened a minimum or a maximum hand. In that case, if you know at what contract you wish to play it, you just up and bid it.

Example:

	partner	opponent	you
	2 ♠	pass	4 ♠
or	2 ♠	pass	3 NT

The beauty of this direct approach in the 2 ♠, 4 ♠ type of sequence, is that the opponents do not know whether you have a strong hand or are merely continuing the preempt. They may wind up making a rash decision, such as doubling your bid when you can safely make it, or overcalling you at a very high level for a disastrous defeat for them.

You will notice that a two club bid is not included in the weak two bid category. The two club opening bid is reserved for use as the "catch-all", *strong, game-forcing two bid.*

The negative response to the opening two club bid is two diamonds, showing a hand containing less than seven high card points. A two no trump response is a *positive* response showing seven or more points. All other responses are positive and natural.

ADVANTAGES AND DISADVANTAGES OF THE OPENING WEAK TWO BID

The Advantages:
1. *Preemptive value:* The opponents have to start competing at a higher level.
2. *Descriptive value:* The weak opening two bid is a limit bid. Partner knows the general strength and texture of your hand in one bid.

The Disadvantages:
1. *It gives up the natural strong two bid.* It forces you to use an artificial two club bid. If the opponents interfere, you may not be able to show your true suit until a much higher level.
2. *It can be dangerous.* You may be doubled and thereby suffer a large penalty, even at a time when the opponents do not have a game.

3. *Not as effective in rubber bridge.* The weak two bid was designed more for duplicate bridge where a ten point scoring swing is significant and the risk of a tremendous set on one deal is not as critical.

4. *It is often misused.* Because they have the weak two bid in their arsenal, some players with a smattering of points and six cards in a suit, feel they must make a bid, when in reality they should pass. On the other hand, some players make opening two bids when a simple one bid is more appropriate.

PREEMPTIVE SINGLE-JUMP OVERCALLS

PREEMPTIVE SINGLE JUMP OVERCALLS

The prime purpose of this bid is to cut down the bidding room of the opponents.

Examples:

	opp't	you
	1 ♡	2 ♠
or	1 ♠	3 ♣

An ideal preemptive jump overcall is one in which the bulk of the high cards are in the bid suit. The suit usually contains six cards. It describes a hand that is essentially similar in strength and texture to an opening weak two bid.

Of course, if you adopt the preemptive single jump over-call into your arsenal of bids, you will have to give up the intermediate jump overcall that we advocated in the earlier part of the book.

It is a fact of bridge life, that every time you add a new convention, tactic or artificial bid you are sacrificing another natural bid or tactic.

Therefore do not add conventions to your system unless you understand them fully.

THE SMARTEST CONVENTIONAL BID Is **DOPI**

ONE OF THE SMARTEST CONVENTIONAL BIDS IS DOPI!

What to do when the opponents interfere with your Blackwood or Gerber ace-asking bid is sensibly solved by a DOPI bid.

Your side is merrily on its way towards slam and the question is how many aces the partnership holds. Partner decides to use the Blackwood convention and bids four no trump.

You are all set to reply when your friendly right hand opponent bids a suit at the five level. What to do? "DOPI" comes to the rescue. DOPI stands for "Double with 0 aces, Pass with 1 ace". It really should read: DOP1.

If you have 2 aces, you bid at the next higher step; with 3 aces, you bid two steps higher; with 4 aces you bid three steps higher.

Here's how DOPI works:

Example: The bidding has gone:

Partner	Opponent	You	Opponent
1 ♠	pass	3 ♠	pass
4 NT	5 ♡	?	

150

A. ♠ K Q 8 7	B. ♠ A K 9 8	C. ♠ A J 7 6
♡ 9	♡ 2	♡ 8 2
◇ K J 9 8	◇ K J 9 7	◇ K J 9 6
♣ K J 10 7	♣ Q 9 8 7	♣ A J 9
Bid: Double	Bid: Pass	Bid 5 ♠

In hand A, with 0 aces you double; in hand B, with 1 ace you pass; in hand C, with 2 aces, you bid one step higher, which in this case is 5 ♠.

The logic of the DOPI method is that it permits you to double the opponents if their interference bid was indiscreet, when a response showing one or no ace is not sufficient for slam. When responder holds two or more aces, the chances are that slam is likely and will be more profitable than setting the opponents.

The Delicate Art of BALANCING

BALANCING

One of the most difficult aspects of bidding is when or how you enter the bidding if the opponents are subsiding at a low level. It requires a delicate touch and a great deal of judgment.

Suppose, for example, the bidding has gone:

opponent	you	opponent	partner
1 ♡	pass	2 ♡	pass
pass	?		

You are now in what is called the balancing position. Do you pass and permit the opponents to play in their 2 ♡ contract? Or do you bid on, competing for the part score?

Here are your considerations.

If competent opponents stop at a low level, it usually indicates that they do not have too many high card points. So your side has some strength too. If your strength is in the opponents' suit or if you have a balanced hand, a good idea is to pass. If you have a good suit of your own, you can overcall. With shortness in the opponents' suit and support for the unbid suits you can double for take-out.

Examples:
After the bidding has gone:

opponent	you	opponent	partner
1 ♡	pass	2 ♡	pass
pass			

What do you bid with these hands?

A. ♠ A 10 8 7	B. ♠ K Q 10 7 6	C. ♠ A 8 7
♡ 4 2	♡ 7 6 3	♡ K J 6
♢ K J 3 2	♢ Q J 2	♢ Q J 4
♣ Q 7 3	♣ 9 2	♣ 10 9 8 7
Bid: Double	Bid: 2 ♠	Bid: Pass

A. You have support for the unbid suits. Double for take-out. B. You have a good spade suit. Bid 2 ♠. C. Though you have good points, your strength is partly in the opponents' suit and scattered elsewhere. Therefore, pass, and hope to defeat the contract.

Vulnerability is an important consideration in deciding whether to bid or pass. If your side is vulnerable and the opponents are not, you are less apt to bid than if the reverse is true.

THIRD HAND OPENINGS

Opening the bidding in third position with *less* than the normal high card strength is often a wise tactic. It is, in a sense, a balancing bid. With two players already passing, the indications are that the high cards are evenly distributed—and your partner may have his fair share of them. (The exception is when the fourth hand has a rock-crusher.)

You may make a third hand opening bid with as few as 9 or 10 high card points if the hand contains a *good suit;* particularly so if it is a major suit. If you don't get your bid in at this juncture, it may be difficult to enter the bidding later.

Also, your opening bid may inhibit the opponents from competing. And if they do get the contract, your partner will know what to lead.

Vulnerability is an important factor in the decision to bid or pass. You may take greater liberties if you are not vulnerable against vulnerable opponents.

Examples:
Your partner and your right hand opponent have passed. What do you bid with these hands?

A. ♠ K Q J 9 5	B. ♠ A K J 7	C. ♠ 6 4 3 2
♡ A 10 3	♡ 9 8 7	♡ A Q 10 9 3
◇ 7 6 5	◇ K 10 6	◇ 8
♣ 5 3	♣ 7 6 3	♣ K 9 2
Bid: 1 ♠	Bid: 1 ♠	Bid: 1 ♡

These are all reasonably sound non-vulnerable third seat openings. Hand A has a very good spade suit. Although Hand B contains only a *four* card spade suit, it is wise to bid it for its preemptive and lead directing values. Hand C contains fewer points, but it has a good heart suit and the length in spades provides some safety against a possible spade contract by the opponents.

Opening the bidding in *Fourth Position* (after three passes) with a sub-minimum hand is another matter. You now know that the high cards are truly equally divided among the four players. A battle for a part score may ensue.

The key to deciding whether or not to open is the spade suit—the top ranking suit. If you "own" the spade suit you are most safe in bidding.

Dorothy Hayden Truscott, the famous international expert, recommends a very interesting "spade" guide line on opening in fourth position. She suggests adding the high card points *plus* the number of spades. If they add up to sixteen or more, it is okay to open.

Examples:

♠ K 9 8 6	♠ 7	♠ A K J 8 7 5
♡ A Q 10 8 7	♡ A Q 10 8 6	♡ Q 9 8
◇ K 4 2	◇ K 9 3 2	◇ 6 3
♣ 7	♣ K 4 2	♣ 4 2
12 points	12 points	10 points
+ 4 spades	+ 1 spade	+ 6 spades
16	13	16
Bid: 1 ♡	Bid: Pass	Bid: 1 ♠

We now return to the partner of the player who opened the bidding in third or fourth position.

Having passed originally, there is no bid that you can make that is absolutely forcing. Therefore, you must be prepared to play the contract in any bid you make. Also, you can't get too excited if you have a pretty good hand. After all, partner may have a sub-minimum hand, and had already taken your strength into consideration when he made his bid.

On the other hand, partner may have made a perfectly sound, full opening bid.

DRURY

Over partner's third or fourth hand opening bid of a major suit, a handy convention to use is "DRURY." (named after Douglas Drury.)

When you originally passed an 11 or 12 point hand, you would normally have to make a jump bid to show that fact. But that might get you overboard, if partner's opening was light. To prevent that possibility, here's how the Drury convention works.

Over partner's 1 ♡ or 1 ♠, you bid 2 ♣, (Drury) which asks partner, "Did you make a *sub-minimum* or a *full* opening bid?"

If it is sub-minimum, he responds 2 ◇. If it is a full opening bid, he may make *any other bid* which describes his hand.

Examples:

You	Opp't.	Ptnr.	Opp't.		You	Opp't.	Ptnr.	Opp't.
Pass	Pass	1♠	Pass		Pass	Pass	1♠	Pass
2♣	Pass	2◇*			2♣	Pass	2♡**	

*A sub-minimum opening bid.

**A full opening bid. In this instance showing a hand with at least five spades and at least four hearts.

Typical hands with which to use the Drury Convention:

♠ J 6 5	♠ 6 3	♠ K 9 8
♡ K J 7 6	♡ A K 6 2	♡ 7 6
◇ K 9 8 6	◇ J 9 8 7	◇ K Q 7 6 5
♣ Q J	♣ K 8 6	♣ K 6 3

You	Opp't.	Ptnr.	Opp't.		You	Opp't.	Ptnr.	Opp't.		You	Opp't.	Ptnr.	Opp't.
Pass	Pass	1 ♡	Pass		Pass	Pass	1 ♠	Pass		Pass	Pass	1 ♠	Pass
2♣					2♣					2♣			

If partner rebids 2 ◇ you return to 2 ♡. With any other rebid, raise to 4 ♡.

If partner rebids 2 ◇, bid 2 ♡. With any other rebid, invite a game contract.

If partner rebids 2 ◇, bid 2 ♠. With any other rebid, raise to 4 ♠.

THE NEGATIVE DOUBLE

This is a bid that requires experience and a delicate touch. Don't use it unless you (and your partner!) are completely comfortable with it and understand it fully.

The Negative Double is a tool that comes in handy when the opponents interfere with your bidding by overcalling.

Here's how it works:

Your partner   right hand opponent   you
1 ♣   1 ♠   ?

What do you bid with this type of hand?

♠ 8 7 5
♡ K J 8 7
♢ A 10 5
♣ 6 3 2

If your right hand opponent had not bid, you would have had no problem. You would have bid 1 ♡. But now what can you do? You're not strong enough to bid 2 ♡. You have only eight points. You can't bid 1 NT, you have no spade stopper. So ordinarily you would pass, and hope that partner could reopen the bidding and you would have another chance to bid.

When playing the "Negative Double" convention, you would double, which would tell partner, "I would have bid if the opponents had not interfered, and I am unable to bid a new suit on my own at the two level." In this particular example it says, "Partner, I have four or more hearts, but am not strong enough to bid a new suit at the two level."

The original purpose of the negative double convention was *not to lose the heart suit*, as a result of the opponent's overcall. It is particularly useful when playing five-card major opening bids.

Like all conventional bids you give up the natural bid at that juncture..."The penalty double."

TRANSFER BIDS

You may recall that in our discussions on no trump bidding
and Stayman, we indicated that it is often wise to have the
opening one or two no trump bidder become the declarer.
The reason behind it is that the no trump bidder has tenace
positions — combinations of cards that are best led up to. The
use of transfer bids helps to accomplish this. The simplified
version of the Jacoby transfer bid is to use it for the major
suits only. It is used when you have five or more cards in a
major suit.

Over partner's opening 1 NT bid, a 2 ◇ bid requires partner to bid 2 ♡ and a 2 ♡ bid requires partner to bid 2 ♠. The
no trump opener winds up bidding your suit, hence the term
"Transfer Bid."

Examples:

Partner	You	or	Partner	You
1 NT	2 ◇		1 NT	2 ♡
2 ♡			2 ♠	

Where you go from there depends upon the strength of
your hand. If you have a hand of seven points or less you

usually pass. With 8 or 9 points and a five-card suit, you rebid two no trump. Partner, *with a minimum hand* and only two cards in your suit, may pass. With three cards in your suit he usually corrects to three in your suit. With a *maximum hand* and two cards in your suit, he bids 3 NT; with three cards in your suit, he usually bids four in your suit.

Examples of hands on which you would use transfer bids: Partner has opened 1 NT.
You hold:

♠ Q J 9 7 6 5	♠ 9 6	♠ 8 3
♡ 9	♡ K J 8 7 3	♡ K Q J 8 6
◇ 9 8 3	◇ A 5 4	◇ 6 5 4
♣ 7 6 5	♣ 6 5 4	♣ A 9 8
Bid: 2 ♡	Bid: 2 ◇	Bid: 2 ◇

Rebids:

Over partner's	Over partner's	Over partner's
2 ♠ bid, pass	2 ♡ bid, bid 2 NT	2 ♡ bid, bid 3 NT

When using transfer bids you can *never* play a hand in a 2 ◇ contract over partner's 1 NT opening. Here again, using a convention gives up a natural bid. Transfer bids can be used over opening 2 NT bids as well, in a like manner, just one level higher.

FLANNERY WILL GET YOU EVERYWHERE...

...IF YOU HOLD FIVE HEARTS AND FOUR SPADES!

FLANNERY: 2 ◇ Opening Bid.

The attempt to handle the difficulty of the rebid on opening hands of minimum strength containing five hearts and four spades can be solved with the use of the Flannery convention.

The Flannery convention can be used if you play weak two

bids. An opening bid of 2 ◇ describes a hand of 11 to 15 high card points containing five hearts and four spades.

Example hands:

♠ K J 9 7	♠ K 9 8 7	♠ K J 6 5
♡ A Q 8 7 6	♡ K Q 9 8 7	♡ A J 10 8 7
◇ J 5	◇ 4	◇ K Q 3
♣ 3 2	♣ A 10 3	♣ 2

Opening bid: 2 ◇.

Partner of the opening Flannery bidder can often place the contract as the opening bid is both descriptive and limited. He can bid 2 ♡ or 2 ♠, 4 ♡ or 4 ♠, or 3 NT. Or he can invite game by bidding 3 ♡ or 3 ♠, asking opener to bid game with a maximum, and pass with a minimum. When responder wishes to probe further, he usually bids 2 NT. The opening bidder responds by showing strength and distribution as follows:

With a 4-5-2-2 distribution: minimum hand (11-13 points) rebid 3 ♡; Maximum hand (14-15 points) rebid 3 ♠.

If the hand contains stoppers in the short suits (example: ♠ A 9 7 6 ♡ K 10 9 8 6 ◇ A 4 ♣ K 6) rebid 3 NT.

With a 4-5-3-1 distribution (3 diamonds) rebid 3 ◇.

With a 4-5-1-3 distribution (3 clubs) rebid 3 ♣.

With a 4-5-0-4 distribution (4 clubs) rebid 4 ♣.

With a 4-5-4-0 distribution (4 diamonds) rebid 4 ◇.

The negative aspects of the Flannery convention are: (1) it gives up the natural weak 2 ◇ bid. (2) If the opposition gets the contract, the hand is an "open book."

We have touched upon some of the methods you will meet as you continue to play in this wonderful world of bridge. They are all treatments and conventions that may be used in conjunction with the so-called "Standard American System."

Of the different styles of bidding that you may encounter, the most important are the "Big Club" systems. The most popular of these is the "Precision Club System."

The main thing to remember when playing against this system is that the 1 ♣ bid is the artificial strong opening bid. It designates a hand which contains *16 or more* high card points. Virtually all other opening bids show *fewer* points. Even a 1 NT opening bid shows only 13 to 15 points. A 2 ♣ opening bid indicates a 12 to 15 point hand with a five or six card club suit.

The responses after the artificial one club opening can become quite complex depending upon the sophistication of the players. All you have to know at the outset is that a 1 ◊ response indicates fewer than eight high card points. All other responses indicate more than that.

If you don't intend to enter the auction, let them go blithely on their complicated way until their bidding is completed. Then, and only then, ask for an explanation of the various bids as a guide to your defense.

All the foregoing should give you an idea of what you may run across as you continue to progress in the world of bridge.

You also have these wonderful additional tools at your command. Select those that you and your partners are comfortable with. Add them slowly in your mix and your bridge batter will be better for it.

As your bridge knowledge and experience increase, you will find that for the greatest enjoyment of the game, the fun way is the best way to serious bridge.